need to know?

# Create
# Your Own
# Website

Michael Gray

Collins

**First published in 2008 by Collins**
an imprint of
HarperCollins Publishers
77–85 Fulham Palace Road
London W6 8JB

**www.collins.co.uk**

Collins is a registered trademark of
HarperCollins Publishers Limited

10  09  08
6  5  4  3  2  1

A catalogue record for this book is available from
the British Library

Produced for Collins by Essential Works Ltd
168a Camden Street, London NW1 9PT
www.essentialworks.co.uk
For Essential Works:
Editors: Nina Sharman and Fiona Screen
Designer: Martin Hendry
Indexer: Hazel Bell

Series design: Mark Thomson
Front cover photograph: © Josh Westrich/
zefa/Corbis
Back cover photograph (middle) courtesy of
www.dogpile.com
Thanks to etre for illustration on page 62

ISBN-13: 978 0 00 726274 8

Colour reproduction by Colourscan, Singapore
Printed and bound by Printing Express Ltd,
Hong Kong

# Contents

# Introduction

There is hardly a business or organization that doesn't have its own website, but if you are the person charged with creating it then the planning, design, uploading and marketing of your web pages can place more than a few obstacles in the way of your internet-publishing dreams. This book aims to share the burden by guiding you through the key stages of website development, from clarifying your needs, to creating templates and graphics and boosting your site's visibility on the major search engines.

The techniques shown are demonstrated using the website of a fictional restaurant, the Camden Canteen. As with all websites, the page you see on screen is the result of some fairly complex-looking computer code, written using Extensible HyperText Markup Language (XHTML) and Cascading Style Sheets (CSS). Though word-processor style software makes it possible to create websites without encountering their underlying code, this book teaches you how to write your site's code manually. This isn't as daunting as it sounds, and you will be rewarded with a much better understanding of website creation – without the need to buy expensive software, or a new computer to run it on. You can see the finished website at www.collins.co.uk/create, where you can also download all the code shown in the book.

At first glance, this book threatens to turn its casual web-using readership into a caffeine-fuelled band of XHTML eggheads and CSS square-eyes. But there is nothing geeky about the sites you'll create. The intention always is to eschew gimmicks for gimmicks' sake and focus instead on techniques that will really make your site easier to create, manage and – most importantly – *use*.

Inevitably, an introductory book like this one can only cover the basics. With this in mind, at the end of each chapter you'll find pointers to where you can learn about specific topics in more detail. Good luck!

# 1 What is a website?

Whether it's online banking, home shopping or catching up on the latest news – browsing the World Wide Web has become part of our daily routine. Yet while we now complete all manner of day-to-day tasks online, what actually lies behind our favourite websites remains, for most of us, something of a puzzle. This chapter aims to demystify the jargon of website creation by breaking a website down into its component parts. You will learn about some of the most common types of website, and identify what kind of site best suits your needs.

# The building blocks

Take a closer look at even the most simple of websites and you will soon see that it is the sum of many different parts. Understanding those parts is the first step towards creating and getting the most out of your own site.

## Content is king

A website without content is not much good to anyone. Content comes in many forms. Text and pictures are the most obvious, but a website can also contain videos, animations, music and other files to download.

Static content is published on a website and does not change until the site owner updates or replaces it. Dynamic content interacts with the person viewing the site, and adapts according to the

The content on the YouTube website is provided by its users who upload their own videos.

individual user. Some sites go one step further and rely almost entirely on the user to provide their content. The video-sharing website, YouTube, is a good example of a site that depends on this kind of user-generated content.

## Presentation perfect

Good content deserves good presentation, and the decisions you make about the way your website looks will play a big part in determining how successful it will be. Your design should reflect the overall tone of your website and present its content in a way that users will instinctively understand. There was a time when web designers' creative ambitions frequently fell foul of technical limitations, but modern technologies are giving web designers greater flexibility than ever before. There's really no excuse for not making an impact!

makeupmakeout.com uses an animated video game to communicate its message of world peace.

**must know**

In modern web design, the files that control how a website looks are kept entirely separate from the site's actual content. As you will discover, this is a highly efficient approach that allows you to make changes to the look of every page of your website quickly and even reformat the same content for different media.

The content on this news site includes text, still images and video clips.

**did you know?**

The Internet Archive Wayback Machine (http://web.archive.org/collections) allows you to view websites as they appeared years ago. It's interesting to see how far online design has come since surfing the web first became a mainstream activity. Compare the 1997 version of Apple's website with the current version, for example, and you can see how high-speed broadband connections have allowed designers to deliver bigger pictures and high-quality video. Notice that the current site is also much wider than its predecessors – a reflection of the trend towards bigger, high-resolution computer screens.

 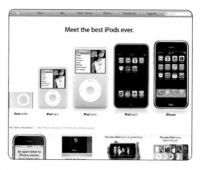

Then and now: the Apple site shows how web design has moved on.

## Are you being served?

Websites live on servers. You can think of a server in much the same way you think of your own computer's hard disk: it's a place to store files until you need them. When you view a website, you are viewing its constituent files on the server where it is stored – just as you view files on your own hard disk. The difference is that the server is in a different physical location to your own hard disk. The Internet allows you to connect to the remote server.

When you set up your own website, you will need to find space for it on a server. Though it is possible to set up your very own server, it's usually better to rent server space from a hosting company for a monthly fee. You'll build your site offline, and then upload it to your server space. Once uploaded, anyone with an Internet connection will be able to visit your site. The server never sleeps: it's ready to serve your website to visitors 24 hours a day.

## Just browsing

Browsers are the software programs that act as middlemen between your website and the people viewing it. You probably already use browsers such as Internet Explorer or Safari to view websites on your own computer, and you might even have used browsers on other devices such as personal digital assistants (PDAs) and mobile phones.

The process of creating a website involves providing browsers with your content and giving them instructions about how you wish that content to be displayed. In this book, Extensible Hypertext Markup Language (XHTML) is used to tell the browser about the content of our website and Cascading Style Sheets (CSS) to communicate the way we wish to present that content.

**A browser is the application software (for example, Internet Explorer or Safari) used to view websites.**

# Types of website

Can you hear that noise? It's probably the inexhaustible hum of the net's latest buzzwords. Separating passing fad from the next big thing can drive even the calmest web designer to distraction, but here are some increasingly popular types of website you should consider.

The database behind this online clothes store organizes products in categories and subcategories.

## Dynamic websites

More and more websites are using databases to store their content. Database-driven sites allow browsers to connect to a web server, whose programs retrieve information from the database and send it to the browser in the form of a web page. Exactly which content is retrieved is decided by individual visitors, who can tailor the request the browser sends to the database according to their own unique circumstances. Imagine the products page of a clothing company's website. Instead of viewing all the clothes the company makes, you could view only the clothes that are available in your size and favourite colour.

Since each user can ask the browser to get different sets of data from the database, the final web page shown must be generated 'on-the-fly' (see glossary page 186). This is why database-driven websites are called dynamic. Dynamic websites can be very powerful, and are also a very effective way of managing content – especially when the same information appears in more than one place.

Most dynamic websites feature a content management system (CMS). The CMS provides a user-friendly way of editing the content on the site's database, using the same web browsers used to view the site itself. Once logged in, website administrators can use the CMS to make changes to the website without having to know anything about the raw computer code that lies behind it.

## Online homepage creation services

Many website hosting companies offer a quick and easy way to create a basic homepage online, using pre-designed templates. If you don't mind having advertisements on your site, services such as Geocities (www.geocities.com) will even create and host your pages for free.

**These two sites were created from Yahoo! Geocities using pre-designed templates.**

**did you know?**

Mac users might want to take a look at Apple's .Mac tools (www.mac.com), which include website creation and hosting services. This certainly isn't the most economical way of creating a website, but it does have the advantage of being designed to integrate well with familiar programs like iPhoto and iMovie.

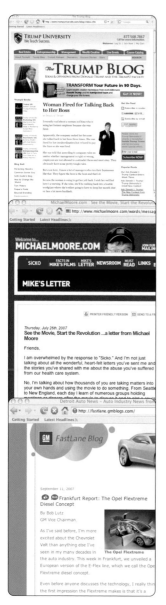

**try this**

Technorati (www.technorati.com) is a search engine that specializes in blogs, and is a great place to sample blogs on topics as diverse as animation and zoology. There are over 70 million to choose from, but if you cannot find what you're looking for try again the next day – according to Technorati, 120,000 new blogs are created every day.

## Blogs

The meteoric rise of the humble blog has taken the Internet by storm. A blog (short for 'web log') is a sort of online diary. Entries are presented in date order, usually organized by topic and with the facility for readers to leave their own comments.

Once the preserve of only the trendiest web citizens, blogs are now big business. Dell, Kodak and McDonald's are just three examples of global brands that have jumped the blogging bandwagon and created their own corporate blogs.

Blogging services make it easy to start and maintain a blog. Some of the most popular include Blogger (www.blogger.com), WordPress (www.wordpress.com) and TypePad (www.typepad.com). All provide ready-made templates you can use to give your blog a professional look without having to design anything yourself. Many blogging services, including Blogger and WordPress, are free.

**From celebrities to political activists and multinational corporations – they all have blogs.**

# Social networking sites

Social networking sites are a new breed of website that allow users to create their own page and link it to those of their friends, thus establishing a social network. Each member's page contains information about the person behind it, and users can also show off their pictures, music and videos.

Sites like MySpace (www.myspace.com), Bebo (www.bebo.com) and Facebook (www.facebook.com) – three of the most popular social networks – are at the cutting edge of popular culture, so it's no surprise that they are awash with pop stars and celebrities. All three will guide you through the process of creating your own profile, and their ready-made templates allow you to change the look of your page at the click of a mouse.

**did you know?**

Social networking sites and blogs are often, controversially, referred to as examples of Web 2.0. Basically the term describes sites that reach out to users in ways that traditional websites cannot, typically fostering a strong sense of virtual community. Other Web 2.0 sites include the social bookmarking site digg (www.digg.com) and the photo-sharing site flickr (www.flickr.com).

Rub shoulders with friends and celebs on social networking sites like Facebook and MySpace.

# What type of site for me?

Identifying which type of website best suits your needs can be a somewhat daunting prospect. Here are some considerations to help you decide.

## Do you need your own website?

You know that you want to be on the web, but what do you want to do when you get there? If you're planning a personal homepage, ask yourself if some of the sites mentioned above can provide the facilities you need. Tasks such as publishing a journal or sharing family photos are easily achieved without having to set up your own bespoke website.

## How much time do you have?

Things move fast on the Internet, and if you needed your website yesterday then catching up could be an uphill struggle. If your host offers an online website creation tool, using its ready-made templates is a great way to get a basic website off the starting blocks quickly. You can always upgrade the site later, replacing the original pages with your own designs.

## How much control do you need?

Sometimes you need things done in a particular way. If you are planning a company website, you will probably want it to match your corporate identity and you certainly will not want other people's names, logos or adverts getting in the way. In this case, developing your own website is likely to be a better option than relying on automated website generation services and ready-made templates.

**must know**

Remember, you cannot do everything yourself. Features such as secure online shops and customized content management systems are beyond the scope of a beginner, so consider getting professional help.

# What's the budget?

Setting up a website can cost anything from virtually nothing to a small fortune. If your budget is nearer the lower end of the scale, make sure you understand any strings attached to services such as free hosting. Is there a support number you can call should you run into problems? A modest investment in a better service could save a lot of heartache later.

If money is no object, be careful not to get carried away. It's easy to dream up all sorts of exciting features for your new website, and most of them will be technically possible. That does not make them a good idea. Make sure that every feature of your site serves a sensible purpose, and resist the temptation to add gimmicks that your target audience will not want to use.

If you fancy a dynamic website with a content management system, ask yourself if you will really make good use of its capabilities. For smaller, infrequently updated sites, the higher development costs of a CMS may outweigh the potential benefits.

# Bandwidth limit

Many hosts limit the amount of data that can be transferred by your site in a given period. This is called the bandwidth limit, and if you exceed it you may be charged. To avoid this, make sure your bandwidth limit is appropriate to your site. The amount you will need depends on how many people visit your site and the size of the files it contains. For example, large numbers of people viewing a video clip use much more bandwidth than a small number of people reading a page of text.

**want to know more?**

• See pages 33-4 for a more detailed discussion of the most popular browsers.
• If you're planning a commercial site, you'll find useful advice at BusinessLink. There's also an interactive questionnaire to help you identify how a website could help you (www.businesslink.gov.uk).
• Familiarize yourself with website jargon (see glossary on pages 186-7).
• For more information and to help you choose the type of website you want, visit www.themcfox.com/the-net

# 2 Getting started

The jargon of website creation has been demystified and the most common types of website have been explained. Now that you are armed with a good idea of what you want from your website, it's time to start developing it. In this chapter, you will learn how to write the code behind your website, find out about useful software, register your own web address and set up a hosting account.

# Anatomy of a web page

XHTML is a programming language used to describe the content of your website. It is easy to write basic XHTML, and with a little background knowledge you can really exploit its full potential.

## About XHTML

XHTML stands for Extensible HyperText Markup Language. It is actually an extension of the older HyperText Markup Language (HTML). The two are very similar, but XHTML boasts compatibility with yet another language, XML. There's no need to worry about XML here, but it's still a good idea to create your website with XHTML as this gives you the discipline to create 'well-formed' documents, that are much more likely to render accurately on the different browsers, both computer- and mobile-based, current and future.

Since HTML and XHTML files are simply coded text, you can open and edit them in a simple text editor such as Notepad on the PC or TextEdit on the Mac.

**must know**

The XHTML code in this book is colour-coded and set out to make it easier to follow. You can, however, write your code in any colour you choose (see key on page 187). See page 72 to find out how to create and save a complete XHTML document.

## First steps in XHTML

At first glance, XHTML code does look pretty daunting. Don't let this put you off though – its grammar is probably more logical than any other language you have ever attempted to master (English included!).

### Let's play tag

XHTML is composed of a series of pre-defined tags, used to denote various types of content. Each piece of content is fully enclosed by the tags applied to it, with an opening tag at the beginning of the content and a closing tag at the end. For example, p denotes a paragraph. To signify the start of a paragraph, you would write <p>, and to close it you would write </p>. Hence the code below produces the paragraph of text shown in the browser window.

```
<p>This is a paragraph of text. The
opening tag tells the browser where the
paragraph begins and the closing tag tells
the browser where it ends.</p>
```

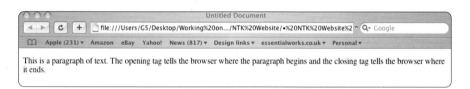

Some tags include extra information in the opening statement, known as attributes. For example, the *a* or anchor tag turns the content inside that tag into a hyperlink to another web page. An attribute called href followed by the equals sign tells the browser the address of the web page to link to:

```
<a href="http://www.collins.co.uk">
Click on this text to visit the Collins
website.</a>
```

Most tags can be placed within other tags. This is known as 'nesting'. For example, we could nest the link created above within the original paragraph of text as follows:

```
<p>This is a paragraph of text.
<a href="http://www.collins.co.uk"> Click
on this text to visit the Collins
website.</a> The opening tag tells the
browser where the paragraph begins and the
closing tag tells the browser where it
ends.</p>
```

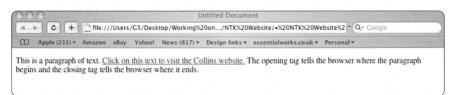

You will learn more XHTML tags in chapter 4.

### Semantically speaking

Good mark-up should be semantic, meaning that it should retain its structure even when stripped of any visual formatting. In practice, this means choosing XHTML tags that are most appropriate to the content they surround. See the following paragraphs:

```
<p>ANATOMY OF A WEB PAGE</p>
<p>XHTML is a programming language used to
organize the content of your website. It's
easy to write basic XHTML, and with a
little background knowledge you can really
exploit its full potential.</p>
```

**must know**

It might seem pedantic, but getting into the semantic habit now will pay dividends later.

The text within the first paragraph looks like the title, as it is written in capital letters. To be semantically correct, however, the title should be enclosed in a true heading tag. In the code below, the h1 tag – the first, top level of heading – is used to tell the browser that the first section of text is in fact a heading:

**The same text displayed with and without a true heading tag.**

```
<h1>Anatomy of a web page</h1>
<p>XHTML is a programming language used to
describe the content of your website. It
is easy to write basic XHTML, and with a
little background knowledge you can really
exploit its full potential.</p>
```

Four key advantages of semantic mark-up are:
• Semantic mark-up makes it easy to make global adjustments to the presentation of the site when all the formatting – such as the capitalization of the heading in the example above – is controlled outside of the individual XHTML pages. That's why the text in the h1 tag above is no longer uppercase in the XHTML code: the case of all h1 headings is a

**On this page from the Victoria & Albert Museum's website, an h 1 title is used for the 'Collections' heading, while h 2 tags enclose the names of each individual collection.**

**did you know?**

When you view a site, the browser shows the result of the page's code. To see the code itself, look for the 'view source' or 'page source' function in your browser's view menu. Viewing the source is an excellent way of improving your understanding of XHTML.

formatting option set in the style sheet. That way, only one change to the style sheet would be required to restyle all h1 headings.

• Semantic mark-up makes it easy to reformat the same content for different media. In the original example above, the title would always have been uppercase. In the revised example, you could use different style sheets to make the title uppercase on a mobile phone, but bold on a computer screen.

• Semantic mark-up is easier for computers – who will, in fact, be an important part of your site's audience – to understand. Search engines use automated 'robots' to trawl the web and index new sites, so semantic code is likely to assure your site a better quality listing. Semantic mark-up is also more easily digested by screen-reading software,

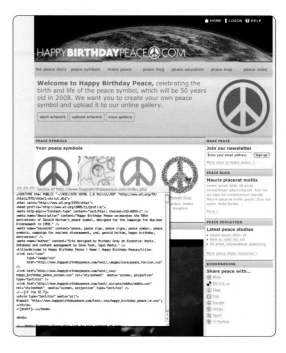

The view source option reveals the code or mark-up behind the page.

which reads the content of web pages aloud to visually impaired users.

- It is easier to write efficient mark-up working semantically. Keeping your code short helps to keep file sizes down, which means users will be able to view your site more quickly, using less of your precious bandwidth quota.

## Validation

When it comes to good grammar and correct usage, the World Wide Web Consortium (W3C for short) is the Internet's answer to the *Collins English Dictionary*. You can use the free W3C Markup Validation Service website to test your code against either a 'transitional' (more lenient) or 'strict' interpretation of current standards, and pinpoint any errors line by line. Pages that have no errors are said to 'validate' or be 'standards-compliant'.

Some web designers question the value of validation, and it's certainly true that many very successful websites are not standards-compliant. Different browsers often interpret the same code in slightly different ways, whether it is valid or not. Nevertheless, the validation process is still a very useful way of highlighting potential problems, and means that your site is more likely to display correctly as new browsers are released.

**must know**

To validate successfully, a web page must declare whether it is to be judged against the transitional or strict standard. Find out how on pages 72–3.

**The W3C Markup Validation Service site – the home of standards-compliant websites.**

**try this**

If you use the Firefox browser, download the web developer toolbar from https://addons.mozilla.org/en-US/firefox/addon/60. It offers lots of useful features, including the ability to validate pages as you look at them.

# Do it in style

Your XHTML may have structure, but you will need to call on the creative abilities of Cascading Style Sheets (CSS) in order to give it some visual appeal.

**The CSS Zen Garden site invites designers to restyle its content with their own CSS file. Visitors choose from the various designs and, though the presentation changes, the mark-up of the content is always the same.**

## About CSS

Before the advent of CSS, information about the formatting of a web page – colours, typefaces, layout and so on – was all contained in the HTML (now XHTML) file. Keeping the formatting information in a separate CSS file, however, is a much better option.

Like XHTML files, CSS files are just coded text, so you can open and edit them in a basic text editor such as Notepad on the PC or TextEdit on the Mac.

### First principles of CSS

The language of a CSS style sheet file is different from that of XHTML, but it is not difficult to pick up once you understand the basic principles.

Think of the style sheet as a rule book which the browser must adhere to when displaying your site. Each rule in the book is called a style, and the elements that the style applies to are called selectors. The details of the rule itself are called declarations, which can consist of a number of formatting properties, each of which has its own value. For example, let's say you wanted to make a rule that all the h1 elements in your XHTML appear in bold, red text. To do this, you would select h1 (your selector), and declare values of red and bold for the color and font-weight properties. The complete piece of code would look like this:

```
h1 {
  color: red;
  font-weight: bold;
}
```

Note that the declaration is enclosed in curly brackets, and that a colon separates a property from its corresponding value. A semi-colon separates each set of property and value. You don't have to use the spaces, line-breaks and tab stops and colours shown above, but doing so makes the code much easier to follow.

There are over a hundred different CSS properties, but in most cases you will only specify a few properties in any one rule. The value of the others is determined by the so-called cascade. This is a hierarchy of rules, where rules higher up the cascade override those underneath. For example, a rule that makes all the text on your page pink would be overridden if a rule for heading text made them yellow. In this case, the rule for the heading text is higher up the cascade because it is more specific than the rule for general text.

You will learn more about CSS in Chapter 5.

**must know**

In this example, the selector is a standard element of the XHTML language and the rule is in fact redefining the styling of that element. Without the CSS, the browser would use its own built-in style sheets to format the h 1 element in its own way. You can also use CSS to format other elements, such as specific pieces of content or types of content. This is covered in greater detail in Chapter 5.

**must know**

The intricacies of the cascade are complex. If a rule you create doesn't seem to work, consider the possibility of its being overridden by another rule elsewhere in your style sheet.

# What software will I need?

You probably already own the basic software needed to create a website, and the programs you do not have are readily available online – many of them for free.

**TextEdit for Mac (left) and Notepad for Windows (right).**

**The code editors BBEdit for Mac (left) and HTML-Kit for Windows.**

**watch out!**

Make sure you save XHTML and CSS files with the correct extension – otherwise the browser will not recognize them as XHTML or CSS, and will simply display the code rather than its result. Save XHTML as either .htm or .html, and CSS with the .css extension.

## Text editors

Since XHTML and CSS are both programming languages, you don't actually need any special software to write them. A basic text editor is all that's required, and you'll find one preinstalled on any computer. If you have a Windows PC, look for the Notepad application. On a Mac, use TextEdit.

## Code editors

Code editors are text editors with extra features designed to help you write error-free code. Code editors typically add colour to the code you type, making it easy to distinguish the different parts of an XHTML element or CSS rule. They can also complete code as you write it, so that you avoid mistakes like opening an XHTML tag without closing it. Leading code editors include BBEdit for the Mac (www.bbedit.com) and HTML-Kit for the PC (www.htmlkit.com).

## WYSIWYG editors

WYSIWYG – or What You See Is What You Get – editors take a different approach. Instead of typing code, you simply add text and graphics to a blank canvas as if you were using a word processor or graphics programme. WYSIWYG editors still produce

XHTML and CSS code, but it's all kept hidden away in the background so you do not have to worry about it.

This may sound like the answer to all your website headaches, but WYSIWYG editors have a patchy reputation. They stand accused of 'codebloat' – producing unnecessarily complicated code that fails validation and eats up bandwidth – and they aren't always flexible enough to realize a page design exactly as the designer envisages it.

The best WYSIWYG editors allow you to tweak the code they generate as you go, thus combining the usability of WYSIWYG with the total control of writing raw code. Adobe Dreamweaver (formerly Macromedia Dreamweaver) is the king of professional WYSIWYG editors (www.adobe.com/dreamweaver), but more affordable options include HotDog PageWiz for the PC (www.sausage.com) and RapidWeaver for the Mac (www.realmacsoftware.com). Amaya is a free, open-source WYSIWYG editor backed by the W3C and available for Windows, Mac and Linux computers (www.w3c.org/amaya).

With WYSIWYG editors, What You See Is What You Get. Or at least, it should be.

**must know**

This book shows you how to create a website using raw XHTML and CSS code. Even if you plan to use a WYSIWYG editor, an understanding of the code is invaluable for tweaking pages and knowing the limitations of what can be achieved.

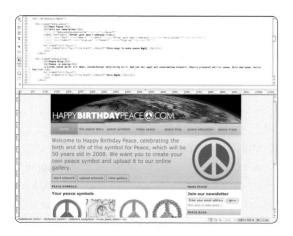

Changes made to the code in the top of half of the window are reflected in the WYSYIWYG display below – and vice versa.

Google founders Larry Page and Sergei Brin used the free Gimp application (right) to create the search engine's ubiquitous multicolour logotype.

# Graphics software

If you plan to include images on your website, you will need a graphics program with which to prepare them. Professional applications like Adobe Photoshop, Adobe Illustrator and Adobe Fireworks are great if you have them, but cheaper options like Adobe Photoshop Elements (www.adobe.com) and Corel PaintShop Pro (www.paintshoppro.com) are more than adequate. These programs are often given away with digital cameras and scanners, so check if you already have a copy. You might also consider Gimp, a sophisticated open-source graphics editor available for free download (go to www.gimp.org).

# FTP clients

FTP (file transfer protocol) is the primary method of transferring your finished website from your own computer to your host's server, using a piece of software called an FTP client. Some WYSIWYG editors boast built-in FTP capability. Otherwise, you will need a separate FTP client. Free FTP clients include SmartFTP for the PC (www.smartftp.com) and RBrowser for the Mac (www.rbrowser.com).

See pages 50–51 for a demonstration of transferring files via FTP.

FTP clients let you upload your site to your host's server.

See pages 50–51 for a demonstration of transferring files via FTP.

## try this

You can find more software recommendations for PC and Mac in the downloads sections of the Microsoft and Apple websites: www.microsoft.com/windows/downloads and www.apple.com/downloads respectively.

It's also worth noting that you can usually download a free trial version of the software from the manufacturer's website.

# Browsers

You could be forgiven for thinking that you only need a browser to view your finished website. In fact, constantly checking the appearance of your site using as many different browsers as possible is a vital – and often infuriating – component of the development process.

The problem is that while all browsers speak the same programming languages, they often seem to have quite different accents. As a result, the appearance of even a standards-compliant web page can vary from browser to browser. Small variations may be acceptable, but in some cases you will have to change the code in order to make sure your site is equally accessible to as many users as possible – regardless of the browser they are using.

### Internet Explorer

Microsoft Internet Explorer (IE for short) comes with all new Windows PCs, so it's no surprise that IE is the world's most common browser. Unfortunately, IE's unique idiosyncrasies can quickly become the bane of a web developer's life. Nonetheless, you should make sure your site works well with the two most recent versions of IE, currently IE6 and IE7. Go to www.microsoft.com/ie to download IE.

### Firefox

Firefox is the challenger to IE's crown, and is the preferred choice of over a third of web users. It is a particularly good idea to test your site in Firefox, as it generally offers a good indication of how other browsers will behave. Go to www.firefox.com to get both PC and Mac versions of Firefox.

**did you know?**

Internet Explorer is no longer available for Mac and you can safely disregard it.

## Safari

Apple's elegant Safari browser is now available for both Mac and PC, so if the success of iTunes is anything to go by, Safari's tiny market share seems certain to rise. Go to www.apple.com/safari to download Safari.

**Originally designed for the Mac, Apple's popular Safari browser, as seen on the PC.**

## Other browsers

Other widely used browsers include Netscape Navigator (www.browser.netscape.com), Opera (www.opera.com) and – for Mac only – Camino (www.caminobrowser.org). Don't forget that internet-capable mobile phones and other mobile devices have browsers all of their own. You can use Opera's Small-Screen Rendering function to preview how your site might look on these devices.

**must know**

New and updated browsers are constantly being released. You can examine the latest browser statistics, updated every month, at www.w3schools.com/ browsers/browsers _stats.asp

# What hardware will I need?

You don't need a top-of-the-range computer to create a top-of-the-range website. The guidelines below will help you determine whether your equipment has got what it takes.

## PC or Mac?

PC and Mac fanatics have been arguing the superiority of their respective computer systems for as long as anyone can remember. You can develop a good website using either system, but whichever you choose you should test your site using both PC and Mac browsers.

Of course, most people only have access to one system. Owners of relatively new Macs are at an advantage, since these models are also capable of running Windows (see www.apple.com/macosx bootcamp for more information). If you have an older Mac or a PC, emulation software such as Virtual PC for Mac and Pear PC provides a way of mimicking another operating system on your

> **try this**
> If you have a PC but don't want to use emulation software to see your site on a Mac, test your site using the PC versions of browsers that are also available for Mac, such as Firefox.

**Are you PC or are you Mac? Well, both, actually.**

**did you know?**
Although you should use the most recent version of browsers, slightly older versions of WYSIWYG editors and graphics software are often good enough. Shop around for discounted software that has been superseded by the latest version.

existing machine (see www.microsoft.com/mac/products/virtualpc/virtualpc.aspx and pearpc.sourceforge.net respectively).

Older Macs can pretend to be PCs using Microsoft's Virtual PC software. Newer Macs can actually run Windows, and software such as Parallels makes it possible to switch easily between the two Windows and Mac operating systems.

## System specifications

Computer programmes don't get much simpler than a basic text editor, and since that's all you really need to write XHTML and CSS files, even older, low-spec computers can still be used to create sophisticated websites.

That said, the modern browsers you will need to test your site do require your computer to meet a certain minimum specification. For example, to install Internet Explorer 7, your PC must have at least a 233MHz processor, 64MB RAM and be running the Windows XP (SP2) operating system. The latest version of Safari for Mac only runs on Macs running Mac OS 10.4.9, which in turn requires at least a G3 processor and 256MB RAM. You can check the system requirements of other software, including WYSIWYG editors and graphics applications, on the manufacturers' websites.

# What's your address?

Look up your home address in the index of a map and you are almost certain to find more than one street with the same name as yours. This is not true of web addresses.

## Talking telephone numbers

You already know that websites are hosted on servers. Every one of these servers has its own unique numerical address, called the Internet Protocol (IP) address.

Internet Protocol addresses are a bit like telephone numbers – and just as difficult to remember. Domain names come to the rescue by translating IP addresses into more palatable combinations of letters and numbers.

**try this**

Enter 209.85.135.147 into your browser's address bar. It's the IP address of a very famous website indeed.

## What's in a domain name?

Although we generally talk about a website's domain name, a website address is in fact formed of at least two domain names, each separated by a dot.

ups.com, denverzoo.org, post.at and srilankan.aero: different top level domains suit different sites.

**must know**

You'll find a full list of top level domains on the website of the Internet Assigned Numbers Authority at www.iana.org

## Top level domains (TLDs)

Every website address ends in a top level domain. The most well-known TLDs are .com, .org and country domains such as .co.uk (United Kingdom) and .de (Germany). There are also a large number of newer, less familiar TLDs such as .aero, .jobs and .mobi. While each of these are aimed at particular types of website, the specific rules about who may use them vary. For example, .org is intended for non-commercial organizations but available to anyone, while .mil is the exclusive preserve of the US military.

The Japanese language site of the computer games company, Sega. Note the Japanese characters in the browser's address bar.

**did you know?**

Internationalized Domain Names (IDNs) are a new type of domain name which can include special characters such as accents, or even be written in non-Roman alphabets. Find out more at www.icann.org/topics/idn

## Second level domains

Every website within one of the top level domains has its own unique second level domain. Second level domains can be made up of any combination of letters and numbers. Spaces are not allowed, but you can use hyphens.

## Subdomains

Subdomains add another level to the hierarchy, appearing to the left of the second level domain. They provide a way of dividing a website into smaller chunks. You can see them in action on the *Guardian* newspaper's website, where the top level domain (www.guardian.co.uk) is divided into various subdomains, commentisfree.guardian.co.uk and jobs.guardian.co.uk being two examples.

Two subdomains of the *Guardian* newspaper's main domain.

# The right address

Choosing domain names can be a tricky business and you may find that the name you want is already in use by another site. Think your options through carefully, as changing your mind later will cost extra time and money. Then, register your choice through a domain name registration agency.

## Do you need a domain name?

Depending on how your website is hosted, it is worth noting that you can still have a site without registering your very own domain name. Free hosting services such as Tripod (www.tripod.com) and GeoCities (www.geocities.com) typically host your website as either a subdomain of their own site or in a folder located within their main domain. The address of your site (its URL, or Uniform Resource Locator) would be in the format yourname.hostsname.com or hostsname.com/yourname respectively.

That said, having your own domain name creates a much more professional impression. Registering your own domain name allows you to choose a memorable web address that doesn't include anybody else's company name, and secures that address for your exclusive use. If you are creating a business website, it is practically a must have. Better still, the registration process is quick and inexpensive.

## Registering a domain name

Domain names are managed by the Internet Corporation for Assigned Names and Numbers

**watch out!**

Don't delay the process of choosing a domain name. If the name you want is available, register it before someone else does!

This website, www.123-reg.co.uk, is an example of a registrar's site.

(ICANN). This is a non-profit organization, which appoints competing private companies as its registrars of domain names. It's worth shopping around to find the registrar offering the best deal on your chosen name, bearing in mind that the range of top level domains on offer may vary from registrar to registrar. Alternatively, check if your hosting company is also a registrar – registering your domain name via the same company that will host the site may be an easier option.

**did you know?**

You can find a complete list of registrars at www.internic.net/regist.html

## Costs

When you register a domain name, you are paying to use that name for a given period of time – generally between one and ten years. At the end of the term, you will need to renew the registration so as to prevent the address being sold to somebody else. The cost of registering a new domain depends on your choice of top level domain, but is usually between £3–£30 a year. You can pay on the registrar's website.

### Availability

Once you've chosen a registrar, go to their website and enter the domain name you're interested in. The site will check to see if that name has already been registered, and if necessary suggest alternatives. If your first choice of name has gone, try and find another option – it is simpler and cheaper than buying a name from the person who already owns it.

**must know**

If you absolutely must have a name that is already registered, find out who the current owner is (go to http://who.is). The owner may be prepared to sell and transfer the name to you.

## Choosing your name

There are lots of factors to consider when you choose a web address. Here are some guidelines to inform your decision.

### Which top level domain?

Although there are now lots of top level domains to choose from, the oldest ones are still the most widely recognized. Choose a TLD to match the content of your site, for example .com for a business or .org for a voluntary organization. Country-specific TLDs like .co.uk are also a good choice, especially if the content of your site is specific to a particular country or language.

Remember that your choice of second level domain is unique only within its top level domain, so www.independent.com and www.independent.co.uk are two entirely separate sites (in this case, the former is a local newspaper in Santa Barbara, California, and the latter is the British daily). Hence

it can be a good idea to register your second level domain under multiple top level domains. You can choose one as your primary address, and set the other addresses to automatically forward visitors to it. This ensures that your site does not get confused with others at similar addresses, and means that people who accidentally enter the wrong top level domain for your website are still directed to your page.

Registering multiple names is also a good idea if you decide to use one of the newer TLDs as your main address. Avoid the temptation to use an unusual TLD simply because your chosen subdomain is not available with a .com or .co.uk ending – you risk losing traffic (see glossary pages 186–7) to the other site.

**www.independent.com and www.independent. co.uk are two completely different sites.**

### Second level domain

For your second level domain, choose a phrase that is pithy and relevant. In theory, the domain can be up to 67 characters long, but you should aim for something short enough to fit neatly on a standard business card.

**Method in the madness? Three sites with unusual names.**

Making the domain name the same as the title of your website is a sensible option. For a business, this means using your company name. In some cases, it might also be appropriate to include the location or type of business. Avoid adding words like 'online' or 'web' as part of your domain name – this was fashionable when the web was in its infancy, but the separation of a business's online and real-world presence now looks increasingly dated.

Domain names which don't at first glance give any clue to the site's business, such as www.amazon.com, offer a good way around the unavailability of more obvious terms, but may need extra promotion before your target audience catches on. Unless you already know that your website is to have an intentionally short shelf-life, look for a domain name with longevity – it is generally not a good idea to change the address of an established site.

Beware any domain name that is difficult to spell or communicate verbally. You don't want to lose visitors because they misunderstood the address you gave them over the phone. Using hyphens can interrupt the flow of a web address when spoken, and there are other ways to separate distinct words in print or on screen.

If you cannot avoid difficult or ambiguous phrases, anticipate user error by registering any obvious misspellings of your core domain name and forwarding visitors to the correct address. For example, customers of the mobile phone operator O2 will still be able to find the company's website, 'www.o2.com', even if they mistakenly enter a 'zero' instead of an 'o'.

Clever typography and use of colour can make the individual words in a website address easier to swallow – without using hyphens.

## And finally, the beginning

Don't forget that your full website address will begin with http://www. Most browsers will add the http:// for you, and in many cases it is not even necessary to type the www. There's a lively but rather technical current debate on the question of whether or not the www. should be part of your address, and in the absence of a consensus the ideal scenario is probably for your site to be accessible both with and without the www. prefix. This is determined by the way in which your hosting is set up, so check with your hosting company.

# Hosting

There is no shortage of companies eager to host your website, and their various hosting packages overflow with features aimed at winning your custom. Here are some things to look out for.

### Disk space and bandwidth

The bigger the files that make up your website, the more space you will need on your host's server. Sites with lots of pictures, sound clips or animations will need the most space, but even a frugal 50mb will be more than sufficient for a basic website. It is easy to buy more room on the server later, so do not pay over the odds for more space than you are ever likely to use.

Do not forget to compare the bandwidth limits of different packages – your host may charge penalty fines if you exceed your allotted bandwidth quota.

**The world's hosting companies compete for your attention.**

## Shared or dedicated hosting?

You'll often find hosting companies offering both shared and dedicated web hosting. This refers to the server that your website will live on. Dedicated hosting means that your site will have a whole server all to itself, whereas shared hosting refers to space on a server that hosts lots of sites together. Shared hosting is perfectly adequate for the vast majority of websites, so don't pay for dedicated hosting unless you know exactly why you need it.

## Windows or Linux?

Another common option refers to the operating system installed on the server that will host your website, usually either Windows or Linux. Though Linux is often said to be more reliable (and is marginally cheaper too), the difference between the two systems only really becomes an issue when you start to develop more advanced, dynamic websites.

Note that this has nothing to do with the operating system you use on your own computer. The process of uploading your site via FTP is the same for both Windows and Linux hosting, so having a Windows PC does not restrict you to Windows hosting.

## Access

The best way to upload your site to the hosting server is via a method known as File Transfer Protocol (FTP). Most hosts offer FTP access, and some also allow you to upload files using your web browser. This latter option can be a useful feature if you need to upload a file but are temporarily unable to connect via FTP.

**must know**

If you wish to create a dynamic site, the programming language you use will be dictated by the operating system of your server. The PHP language is used for databases on Linux servers (though it runs on Windows too), whereas ASP and ASP.net are used on Windows servers. PHP is an open-source language; it is developed by voluntary developers and made available freely. ASP and ASP.net are developed by Microsoft.

**An example of a typical control panel, which you can access via your web browser.**

Most hosts provide a so-called control panel for you to manage your account. Log in to your control panel via your web browser.

## Email

Most hosts allow you to set up email accounts using the same domain as your website. If you are creating a business website, having matching email addresses is a big bonus. Look out for POP3 or IMAP access to your email, as this allows you to retrieve and compose messages using an email programme such as Outlook Express or Apple Mail. You should also be able to access your email via a web browser. This feature – called Webmail – means you can keep up to date with your messages even when you're not at your own computer.

## Site statistics

Want to know how many people visited your site last week? Questions like this are answered by the site's visitor statistics, and the statistics packages offered by many hosting companies display this data in an easy-to-understand graphical format, viewed through your browser. Statistics can be a powerful way to quantify the success of your site, but if your host doesn't provide them don't worry – there are other ways to collect the same information without spending extra money.

## Support and reliability

Find out whom to contact if you run into difficulties managing your hosting, and browse the company's online support pages to get an idea of the help on offer. If there is a telephone helpline, find out how

**must know**

Don't feel you have to choose a hosting company based in your own home country. The internet is a global medium, and as long as the hosting server is reliable and well maintained, its physical location should make little difference.

much the calls will cost and check the opening times. It's usually easier to fix a problem when you are sitting in front of your computer, so make sure that the helpdesk hours suit your schedule.

It takes a lot of work to create a really good website, and you do not want the fruits of your labour to be offline if your host is having technical difficulties. Look for a host with robust back-up systems and seek personal recommendations. The user forums on sites such as www.uk.tophosts.com can be informative, but note that people are more likely to contribute negatively rather than positively.

**watch out!**
Always keep your own back-up copy of your website. If your host becomes unreachable, you may need it!

## Free stuff

Lots of hosting companies throw in free software to help you design your site. Do not overestimate the value of the goods on offer. There are plenty of inexpensive or even free software packages available elsewhere. If you do want to use your host's software, make sure it is compatible with your computer.

Similarly, online site generation tools may come in handy at first, but are likely to become inadequate as your knowledge of site development grows.

Other giveaways include free images and vouchers to advertise your site on the major search engines.

**did you know?**
If you intend to develop your site further, it is worth looking out for more advanced features. Support for FrontPage extensions will be useful if you plan to design your site using Microsoft's FrontPage software, and the ability to install CGI scripts may be desirable.

## More advanced features

A whole range of advanced features have become increasingly common components of affordable web hosting. These include the ability to create dynamic database-driven websites using technologies such as PHP, MySQL and ASP as well as integration with blog services such as WordPress and even online shopping.

# Connecting to your host via FTP

When you set up a hosting account, your host should provide all the details you need to connect to your site via FTP. Here RBrowser on the Mac is used to connect to our server space, but the process is similar whichever FTP client you use.

## Using an FTP site

**1** Open your FTP client and select new site to create a new connection.

**2** Under protocol, choose FTP (not Public FTP).

**3** Enter the address of your website in the Host URL box, not including the www domain. In some cases, you will need to enter the IP address of your site instead – check the information supplied by your host.

**4** Enter your username in the appropriate box, and then your password. Your password will appear as a series of dots or stars – don't worry, this is just to prevent anyone standing over your shoulder from seeing what you are typing.

**5** The other details can usually be left blank. Click the login button to connect to your server space in the main window.

**6** Depending on your host, some folders may already have been created for your files. In most cases, the files for your website belong in the folder called public_html. When you have created your website, you will drag it from your machine and drop it into this folder.

**must know**

You should name the homepage of your site either index.html, index.htm, default.html or default.htm (depending on your host's instructions). This is the page that appears when your main web address, such as www.youraddress.com, is entered into a browser.

**want to know more?**

• Plenty of web pages offer advice on choosing domain names, such as http://www.tamingthe beast.net/articles/what sinaname1.htm
• For more on whether to include the www. prefix in your site address, see no-www.org
• You can use a graphics program to create a quick mock-up of a web page design before you start developing the code. See page 66 for more details.
• For more detailed information on how to organize your files, see pages 68–9 in Chapter 3.
• See pages 165–71 to learn more about website statistics.

# SITEMAP

home

about     products

contact     history     crayons     pencils

# COLOUR

#9966FF     #FF33FF     #CC99CC

#FF9900     #FFCC00

# 3 Planning your site

The web makes things available instantly, and you may already be feeling a strong sense of urgency to get your website online at the earliest possible opportunity. Unfortunately, it's all too easy to churn out an ill-conceived site that's overflowing with technological wizardry but utterly devoid of useful, easily accessible content. This section explores how people are really likely to use your site, and shows you how to plan its structure and presentation.

# Putting the user first

Websites come in endless varieties, but common to them all is the fact that they are an interface with people. Failing to plan for the way your target audience will use your site risks turning all the effort of creating it into an essentially fruitless exercise.

On www.lego.com, a large amount of content is divided into three main sections. There are links to each section at the top of every page.

## Websites are not leaflets or books

A website can be a superb marketing tool and is often a lot cheaper to produce than traditional printed material, but do not fall into the trap of planning your site in the same way you might structure a printed document.

### Structure

While you can fairly assume that readers of a book or brochure will start from the beginning, the same does not apply to website visitors. The vast majority of users will find your site via a search engine like Google, and the search result they click on is very likely to lead to a page deep within your site – not your main homepage. In order for visitors to be able to move around your site, you must include links to its main sections on every page. You should aim to use a consistent basic page template across the whole site, so that users only have to familiarize themselves with one system of getting around.

Keep the navigation of your website simple, and ensure that the names of the different sections and pages are as clear to others as they are to you. If there are specific tasks that you want visitors to your site to complete – for example, viewing a particularly important piece of information or completing an

online form – ensure that the relevant pages are accorded suitable prominence.

Most visitors will take only a few seconds to decide whether a web page deserves their continued attention, so don't bury important information in unnecessary waffle. Instead, break text into bite-size chunks and use relevant keywords for headings. Remember that the user will have to scroll down to see all the content of a very long page, so try to spare them this effort by getting to the point as quickly as possible.

Google's minimalist homepage gets straight to the point. The other examples here are a little less minimalist, but still direct the user's attention effectively.

## Presentation

When a business sends a customer a brochure, the customer sees the brochure exactly as its designer conceived it. Since different browsers can display the same site in slightly different ways, web designers don't get the same kind of control. This can be infuriating, but it is also an opportunity to optimize

**must know**

The advice here not only makes your website more useful for humans, but also helps search engines such as Google understand your site, which means that your site or pages should appear high up in any search results.

The layout of this web page doesn't fall apart when the user makes the text bigger.

the presentation of your site for the varying needs of different users. For example, it is easy to let users make the text of your website bigger. This is a really useful feature, so don't design pages that depend on text being a certain size to look good. From text size to colour and layout, you should aim to put usability at the centre of all your design decisions.

## must know

Very old browsers have little or no understanding of CSS, but can still make sense of well-structured XHTML. Writing good XHTML for such a scenario is a good example of what is called 'graceful degradation'. This is an important part of accessible web design, which focuses on creating sites that can adapt to the widest possible range of audiences.

### Technical considerations

Human nature plays a big role in the way people will use your website, but it is also important to think about the software and computer they will be using to access it. Making sure that your site works with the browsers recommended in the previous chapter is a good start, but you will need to test more extensively if your site is to work with software such as screen-readers, older browsers and mobile-phone browsers. Older monitors cannot display as many colours as newer screens.

Don't forget that a high-speed broadband connection is still a dream for many users. Even broadband users quickly lose patience with sites that take more than ten seconds to load, so don't make visitors wait for overly large files.

## Creating a sitemap

The next step is to sketch out the structure of your site in a hierarchical diagram called a sitemap. It works a bit like a family tree, dividing your site into its component pages and showing how the different pages relate to each other.

Many WYSIWYG editors and numerous dedicated sitemap programmes will create a sitemap for you, but a pen and paper is all you really need to get started. The sketch below shows the sitemap of our fictional restaurant website, Camden Canteen.

The homepage, at the top of the tree, is the main page of our site, the one that appears when a user enters the restaurant's web address into their

The sitemap for the Camden Canteen sample website.

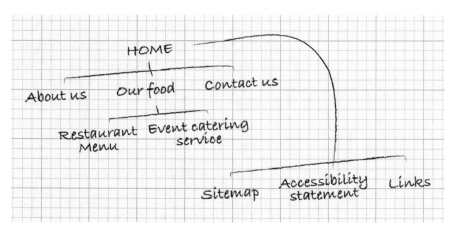

**try this**

Show your sitemap and mockup to impartial outsiders. See what kind of information they look for, and how long it takes them to find it. You can also get ideas from other websites, so visit similar sites to see what they are doing - what

does and doesn't work. Your findings may surprise you, but don't be deterred from going back to the drawing board, if necessary - extra time spent fine-tuning the sitemap at this stage will pay dividends later.

browser. Then, the site is divided into three main sections: a page about the restaurant, a page about its food and a page to contact the restaurant. The food section is further divided into a page showing the restaurant's menu and a page with information on its private catering service. Finally, there are four pages of non-core content that sit outside any of the main sections, including a page of links to other sites and an online version of the sitemap to help users find their way around.

Exactly how your website is structured will depend on its particular content and objectives. What is important is that the sitemap should be easily understood by anyone who visits or maintains the site, and flexible enough to be expanded as your site grows. It will always be easy to add extra sections and pages, but you don't want to be renaming and restructuring existing content in order to accommodate new material logically. Think carefully about the kinds of pages you might want to add later, and make sure that your initial structure leaves room for them.

# Design options

With the user in mind and a solid sitemap before you, it's time to think about the layout and visual appearance of your website. Researching other sites helps to get an idea of your options.

## Layout types

Have you ever noticed how some websites always fill the whole width of your browser window, while others take up the same amount of space no matter how much you resize your window? This behaviour is down to the way the site is designed.

### Fixed layouts

A fixed layout is one where the width of a page is measured in a fixed number of screen pixels. Most modern screens have a resolution of 1024 pixels wide by 768 pixels high, so a website with a fixed width of 800 pixels would take up just over three quarters of the screen width. At a screen resolution of 800 by 600 pixels, however, the user would have

**must know**

For screen resolutions, check the latest statistics on web users' screen resolutions at www.w3schools.com/browsers/browsers_display.asp

**The BBC site uses a fixed-width layout. It fits neatly on an 800 by 600 pixel screen – at 1024 by 768 pixels, there's room to spare.**

This website design requires a fixed layout so that the text will also remain within the frame created by the picture at the top of the page.

The website of Roy's Restaurant, Hawaii.

The website of Buen Ayre, London.

to make their browser window fill the entire width of the screen to view the complete width of the same page without scrolling (see illustrations).

Designers typically choose a fixed width layout when working with designs that rely on precisely positioned graphics. So-called 'pixel perfect' designs do not display correctly if tight control over the page dimensions is relinquished. On the website of Roy's Restaurant, Hawaii (www.roysrestaurant.com), the main content is just 415 pixels wide, and any leftover space in the browser window is filled with the page's background colour. In this case, the content is positioned in the top left of the browser window, but the fixed width area can also be made to float in the middle of the screen, so that it appears to slide back and forth as the browser window is resized. Buen Ayre, an Argentinean restaurant in London, uses this technique on its website (www.buenayre.co.uk).

Fixed-width layouts are extremely popular. However, you should bear in mind their limited flexibility. If you do choose a fixed width design, remember that the resolution of your screen will not always be the same as that of your site's visitors.

**Fluid layout**

In a fluid layout, a web page's dimensions are specified not in finite numbers of pixels but in relative units, such as a percentage of the overall browser window width. If a page is given a width of 100 per cent, it will always fill the entire width of the browser screen, regardless of the user's screen resolution. Fluid layouts are therefore much better at adapting to different users than fixed width designs. For example, while users with relatively small screens might have to scroll horizontally to see a wide fixed-width design in full, a fluid design would contract to fit the available space.

Fluid designs – sometimes also known as liquid layouts – are most popular on blogs and other text-heavy sites, where the exact positioning of images is less critical. For example, the NHS Choices site (www.nhs.uk) has a fluid 100 per cent page width,

**This is a fluid design: when the browser window is resized, the elements of the page change shape to fit the space available.**

Companies such as etre (www.etre.com) provide heat maps of individual websites, showing the most viewed areas of the screen. Black areas – like the parts of this page that are not visible without scrolling – attract hardly any attention.

which contains three columns. The width of each column is set to be just under a third of the available screen space. Added together, they will always fill the entire browser window, contracting and expanding to fit.

Truly fluid layouts – where all dimensions are specified in relative units – require careful thought, but the accessibility benefits are worth the effort.

## Division decisions

Notice how websites divide different bits of content into different areas of the web page, and think about the areas you might need to define in your basic template. You can divide your page into an endless number of horizontal and vertical divisions, but try to choose your layout purposefully – there's little to be gained from an unnecessarily complex design.

Deciding what goes where is not to be taken lightly. Remember that most users will scan over your page before deciding whether to view it in more detail, so make sure that pertinent information will not escape their initial glance.

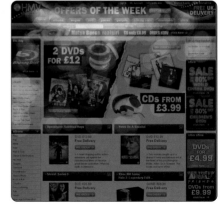

The graphic on the previous page is a heat map of a web page, showing the areas of this web page we most incline towards viewing in increasingly bright shades. The black areas are cold – they hardly attract our attention at all.

## The name of your site
Don't forget that search engines and other websites can send users to any page of your site, so you will need to announce the name of your site on every page. Most sites include their name or logo across the top of the page, or in the top left-hand corner.

## Navigation
Navigation links on every page of your website allow users to get around the site easily. Most sites position these links either across the top of every page or down the left-hand side of the screen. Larger sites often have two levels of navigation: the primary navigation links to the main sections of a site, while the secondary navigation contains links to the pages within each section. Links to functional pages such as the sitemap or search page are often given a space all to themselves, outside the main navigation.

The Denver Museum of Art site uses an attractive colour-coded menu system for its primary and secondary navigation.

### watch out!
For now, avoid navigation menus that unfold different options as you move your mouse over them. Although they can be useful in very large sites, getting these menus to work reliably in all browsers is a task best left for more advanced developers!

## Main content

The main content of every page will normally take up the most screen space. Do not attempt to run text in newspaper-style columns – having to scroll up and down like a yo-yo is sure to irritate users.

## Advertisements

If you expect to have advertising on your site, you will need to leave space for the most popular advert sizes. 'Banner' adverts typically appear at the top of the page, to the right of a site's logo, while vertical 'skyscraper' adverts are used down a column next to the main text.

## Footers

Many websites use a footer at the bottom of every page for items such as copyright declarations, contact details and links to a site's privacy policy, accessibility statement and sitemap.

**The layout of this page leaves room for advertisements above and around the main content.**

**Ma grand-mère fait de la radio**
Un sujet qui tient ses promesses :
Adèle, 80 ans, recopie des cassettes
audio sur lesquelles sont enregistrés
ses souvenirs et ses petits-enfants.
☐ Ecouter

**René Bousquet ou le grand
arrangement** - Un film sans
concession qui éclaire les silences et
les compromis passés à la Libération.
Avec Daniel Prévost, parfaitement
glacial.
☐ Téléchargement locatif / définitif

**Loft / Door III - Coffret 2 DVD**
de Kiyoshi Kurosawa
Deux thrillers torturés dans la veine
fantastique du maître japonais.
☐ Acheter le DVD

# Design style

Behind the code, a lot of creative decisions go into producing the best websites. Look out for colour combinations, illustration styles, typography and layouts to inspire your own site.

Ultimately, the final appearance of your site should reflect its purpose. It is perfectly acceptable for your personal homepage to look like the virtual equivalent of a teenager's bedroom, but a professional site will require a more disciplined approach. If your company already has a logo or house style, design your website to match. Alternatively, you could use the creation of your company's website as a chance to refresh its overall visual identity.

The footer on the website of the Franco-German television network Arte repeats the site's main navigation options and links to useful secondary information, including the channel's contact details and privacy statement.

# Creating a mock-up

A mock-up of your basic template offers a quick way to visualize your website design without getting bogged down in code.

### How to draw a mock-up

It's both quicker and easier to sketch out your initial layout ideas for your website on paper. Start by drawing out boxes for the different divisions of content. You should add colour and detail only when you are satisfied with the basic shape of your page.

Next, either carry on working on paper, or use a graphics application to create your mock-up on screen. The mock-up below was designed using Photoshop, but any graphics programme with which you are familiar will do.

The Camden Canteen is our fictional online restaurant (see page 57 for a sitemap of the Canteen). It has a simple structure and is designed to be straightforward both to create and to use.

**Sketch out rough layouts before you get bogged down in details like colour and wording.**

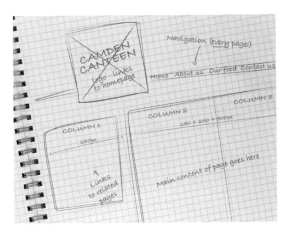

The logo appears in the top left-hand corner of every page.

This is a fixed layout. The main content is 750 pixels wide, which will still fit on older 800 by 600 pixel screens, and sits in the middle of the browser window.

The space below the navigation is divided into three columns, each 210-pixels wide. The main content will run over the middle and right-hand columns, while the left-hand column can be used for secondary information such as pointers to related pages.

There is room for banner and skyscraper ads, in case these need to be added later.

Our site is simple, so we have only one level of navigation, which runs across the top of the page. There are links to all the main sections of the site, and the section currently being viewed is highlighted.

The footer includes a copyright statement and two non-core links.

The margins to the left and right of the three main content columns are 20 pixels each, so the two margins, three columns and two gutters correctly add up to a total width of 750 pixels. Using a common grid to structure your page designs creates well-balanced layouts that bear a pleasing family resemblance to one another.

# Prepare to start coding

You are almost ready to start coding your website. To work efficiently, however, you will need to get organized first.

## How you will work

Static websites are usually created and tested on the designer's computer before they are uploaded to the host server. In order for the links between different files to work consistently, it is essential that their final location in relation to each other on the host server be mirrored exactly on your own computer.

## How to organize your files

Begin by creating a folder on your hard disk, and name it after your website. Inside this folder, create two more folders. Use one to store documents that are related to your site, but which will not actually form part of the site itself. This could include your mock-up, as well as draft copy and research notes. Use the second one for the site itself, adding further folders within it as described below.

**must know**

The folders will contain all the XHTML documents in each section of the site. Name the main page of each either index.htm, index.html, default.htm or default.html. This page will display when the user appends the folder name to the address of your site (for example www.yoursite.com/contact). This is an easy way to direct people to specific parts of your site, so choose folder names with this in mind.

| | Camden Canteen website | | |
|---|---|---|---|
| Name ▼ | Date Modified | Size | Kind |
| ▼ 🗁 Website | Today, 11:18 | -- | Folder |
| ▶ 🗁 sitemap | Today, 11:16 | -- | Folder |
| ▶ 🗁 search | Today, 11:16 | -- | Folder |
| ▶ 🗁 links | Today, 11:16 | -- | Folder |
| ▶ 🗁 food | Today, 11:13 | -- | Folder |
| ▶ 🗁 contact | Today, 11:13 | -- | Folder |
| ▶ 🗁 accessibility | Today, 11:16 | -- | Folder |
| ▶ 🗁 about | Today, 11:13 | -- | Folder |
| ▼ 🗁 _images | Today, 11:18 | -- | Folder |
| ▶ 🗁 sitemap | Today, 11:16 | -- | Folder |
| ▶ 🗁 search | Today, 11:16 | -- | Folder |
| ▶ 🗁 links | Today, 11:16 | -- | Folder |
| ▶ 🗁 food | Today, 11:13 | -- | Folder |
| ▶ 🗁 contact | Today, 11:13 | -- | Folder |
| ▶ 🗁 accessibility | Today, 11:16 | -- | Folder |
| ▶ 🗁 about | Today, 11:13 | -- | Folder |
| ▼ 🗁 _css | Today, 11:16 | -- | Folder |
| ▼ 🗁 Other | Today, 11:14 | -- | Folder |
| ▼ 🗁 Research | Today, 11:15 | -- | Folder |
| 🗋 Website ideas.doc | Today, 11:15 | 20 KB | Microsoft Word document |
| ▼ 🗁 Mockup | Today, 11:18 | -- | Folder |
| 🗋 Camden Canteen mockup.psd | Today, 09:58 | 41.4 MB | Adobe Photoshop file |

**This window shows the complete folder structure for our site.**

## Folders for each section

Go back to your sitemap and create a separate
folder within your site folder for each section of
your site. You will store all the XHTML files for each
section in their respective folders. For our sitemap,
we have created section folders called 'about' (for
the about us section), 'food' (for the our food
section) and 'contact' (for the contact us section).
To keep things tidy, we've also put the links page,
search page, accessibility statement and sitemap
in folders named 'links', 'search', 'accessibility'
and 'sitemap' respectively.

## Images folder

Create another folder within your site folder for all
the graphics used on your site. You may wish to
subdivide this into additional folders for each
section of your site, matching those that you have
already created for the XHTML files.

## CSS folder

Next, create another folder within your site folder
in which to store the cascading style sheets. Now
you're all set to start writing your website's code.

# 4  Using XHTML

You have learnt how websites work and have a pretty good idea of the site that you would like for yourself. Your server space is ready and waiting, and you have armed yourself with more web browsers, code editors and FTP clients than you ever thought existed. But you still only have a mock-up of your future website. In this chapter, you will start writing the code you need to turn your mock-up into a fully functioning web page.

# Creating an XHTML document

The first step is to create an XHTML page that replicates the divisions of content in your mock-up. This will be the basis of a template, which you can reuse for every page of your site.

## Open and save your document

Use your text, code or WYSIWYG editor to open a new blank document and save it with either a .htm or .html file extension. Name this template anything you like, but you might like to save it in a separate templates subfolder of your main website folder.

We are using the code editor built into the Dreamweaver application, but you will get the same result using other code editors or basic text editors such as Notepad (PC) or TextEdit (Mac). If you are using a basic text editor, check the program's settings to ensure that files are saved in Plain Text format. Files saved in Rich Text format will not be read as XHTML by browsers. Note that text editors will not colour code or anticipate what you are typing like code editors do.

## Anatomy of an XHTML file

XHTML files are divided into two sections, each enclosed in a special XHTML tag and both nested within yet another XHTML tag. Before all this, the document type tag declares what kind of XHTML code the rest of the file contains.

### Declaring the doctype

You already know that you can validate your code according to different standards of XHTML, and it's

**must know**

You can save your file in the WYSIWYG editor's native template format. In Dreamweaver, save templates with the .dwt file extension. You will need to identify areas of editable content within your template. When you start a new page based on the template, only these areas can be changed. Amendments to the non-editable areas should be made to the template file itself, and the WYSIWYG editor updates all pages based on the template automatically.

the document type (doctype) tag that tells both the validation service and, more importantly, visiting browsers which interpretation of XHTML your page aspires to.

Browsers will interpret the rest of your XHTML according to the doctype you declare, so the declaration should be the first line of XHTML code you write. It's usually best to choose a 'strict' doctype. This is the most stringent application of web standards. Using it should make your site more likely to display correctly in future versions of web browsers, assuming that these will become increasingly standards-compliant themselves. The code for a strict XHTML doctype looks like this:

**must know**

'Transitional' doctypes result in a more forgiving interpretation of current standards. They are useful if you cannot avoid using certain 'depreciated' code – tags that were once compliant with a strict doctype, but which have since been phased out. There is an example of this on page 85.

```
<!DOCTYPE html PUBLIC "-//W3C//DTD XHTML
1.0 Strict//EN"
"http://www.w3.org/TR/xhtml1/DTD/
xhtml1-strict.dtd">
```

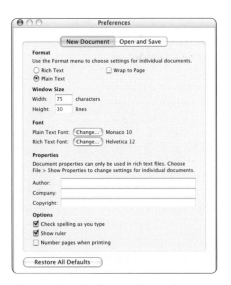

**When opening and saving your document (XHTML), this is what you will see.**

**If you're using a basic text editor, make sure files are saved as plain text.**

## HTML element

After the doctype, open and close an element called HTML as follows:

```
<html xmlns="http://www.w3.org/1999/xhtml"
xml:lang="en" lang= "en"></html>
```

The attributes shown here are to do with XML rather than XHTML, so we don't need to worry too much about them. In fact, all you really need to know about the HTML element is that the rest of your code should be written in-between the opening and closing HTML tags.

## Head element

This is the first element to go between the opening and closing HTML tags. At first glance, the code in the head element does not appear to generate any visible result when you load your page in a browser. Do not be deceived – you will be storing some very important information here. To get started, open and close an element called title within the head tags as follows:

```
<head>
  <title></title>
</head>
```

Inside the title tag, give your page a descriptive title. You can use words, numbers and spaces.

```
<title>My first web page</title>
```

When you open your page in a browser, its title is displayed in the title bar of the browser window. The

**did you know?**

The exclamation mark in the doctype code indicates that this is a particularly important piece of code.

text you enter between the title tags is one of the most important factors in determining how your page is rated by search engines, and it is important to give every page of your website a unique and relevant title.

## Body element

The body element contains the code behind everything you see in the main browser window. Open the body element after the closing tag of the head element, and close it before the closing HTML tag. It's traditional to write 'Hello, World!' as a test message, shown here in a paragraph:

```
<!DOCTYPE html PUBLIC "-//W3C//DTD XHTML
1.0 Strict//EN"
"http://www.w3.org/TR/xhtml1/DTD/xhtml1-
strict.dtd">
<html xmlns="http://www.w3.org/1999/xhtml"
xml:lang="en" lang="en">
<head>
  <title>My first web page</title>
</head>
  <body>
    <p>Hello, World!</p>
  </body>
</html>
```

To see the page this code generates, close the file in your editor and open it in a web browser instead. It should look like the screen shot opposite, with the title in the browser's title bar. If it doesn't, go back to your code and check for typos.

**must know**

Remember that the line breaks, indents and colours used here have no effect on the way the page is displayed – they just make the code easier to manage. As far as the browser is concerned, you could just as well write all the code in one colour and on one line.

The content contained in the body section of the XHTML document is shown in the main browser window and the text entered between the title tags of the head section appears in the window's title bar.

# Adding structured content

You have now got a working XHTML file. The next stage is to start adding the content you included in your mock-up, starting with the main content.

## Heading levels

In a well-structured XHTML document, content should be broken down under a series of different headings. These headings are hierarchical, arranged in six levels of decreasing importance. Thus a top level heading is surrounded by <h1> and </h1> tags, while the next most important heading is surrounded by <h2> and <h2> tags – continuing all the way down to <h6> and <h6>. Paragraph tags – the <p> and </p> we used around Hello, World! – are still used around each paragraph of text beneath the various headings.

**Master your headings**

**1** Go back to your XHTML file, and change the paragraph tags around 'Hello, World!' to <h1> and </h1>. It's a good idea to make the name of your site the top heading on every page, so delete 'Hello, World!' and enter your site's name instead.

**2** The next most important heading in this design is the name of the page. On a new line of code, type the name of a dummy page and enclose it in <h2> and </h2> tags. As this document will serve as a template, you can change the text between these tags each time you create a new page.

**3** Now add the text for your page, enclosing each individual paragraph in **<p>** and **</p>** tags. Again, you can use dummy text for the template and replace it with real copy for each page you create.

**4** To break the text down into more manageable chunks, add some subheadings using **<h3>** and **</h3>** tags. You can have more than one heading at the same level.

**5** If you need them, add extra heading levels. The lowest possible heading level tags are **<h6>** and **</h6>**.

> **did you know?**
>
> If you are using a WYSIWYG editor, look for a 'preview in browser' command to open your page in different browsers.

## Preview and test your code so far

Get into the habit of testing your code in the main web browsers regularly. It is much easier to fix a problem if you know exactly what has changed since your page last displayed correctly. Select 'Open' in the File menu of each browser to locate your XHTML file and open it in the browser window.

Remember to preview and test your code at regular intervals as you go.

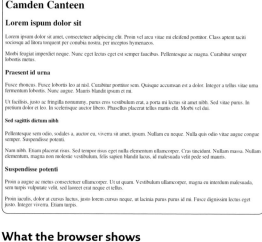

## What the browser shows

The browser has taken the text you entered between the different heading and paragraph tags, and formatted it accordingly. You can clearly see the hierarchical structure of the document in action. Remember that you have not yet used CSS to specify any particular formatting options, so the browser is falling back on its own default settings for colours, fonts and type sizes. Although these defaults might not be very exciting, it is important to see that the page still makes sense as pure XHTML – that way, you can be sure that search engine robots and users of browsers and screen readers that don't use CSS will still be able to use your website.

## Trouble-shooting and validation

It is also a good idea to validate your code frequently, even if things appear to be working correctly. The W3C's web-based Markup Validation Service checks your code for any errors lurking deep within it.

**did you know?**

If you are using the web developer toolbar in Firefox, choose 'Display Page Validation' from the 'Tools' drop-down menu to validate the page without visiting the Markup Validation Service site directly.

## Using the W3C Markup Validation Service

**1** You will find the HTML and XHTML validator at www.validator.w3.org

**2** The tabs at the top of the page give you three ways to validate your code: if your page is already online, you can simply enter its URL. Alternatively, you can upload the entire page from your hard disk or copy and paste chunks of code manually using the 'Validate by Direct Input' option.

**3** Once you have submitted your code, click the 'Check' button. The validator will examine your handiwork, and list any errors. In this case, we've started an **<h1>** heading but used the wrong closing tag at the end. The validator shows exactly which line the problem occurs on, making it easy to locate in our code.

**4** When you've fixed the error, click the 'Revalidate' button to check the page again. If the page validates, you will see a success message on a green background.

# Adding navigation

The navigation links on every page are crucial – without them, users will not be able to get from one page of your site to another. A good, semantic way to describe your navigation device in XHTML is as an unordered list of links.

### Divide and rule

The most logical moment for users to be presented with the main navigation device comes after they have read the name of the site (in this case, Camden Canteen), but before the main content of the page they are currently looking at. To achieve this, it is sensible to section off the different areas of our code according to the different areas of content shown on our visual mock-up. The `<div>` element makes it easy to create these divisions. In the code shown here, `<div>` and `</div>` are used to create five initial divisions: one for the header area (containing our existing top level heading),

**must know**

Remember you can download all the code and graphics featured in this book at www.collins. co.uk/create

```
                                    basic_template.html (XHTML)*
  Code    Split    Design   Title: Camden Canteen

1   <!DOCTYPE html PUBLIC "-//W3C//DTD XHTML 1.0 Strict//EN" "http://www.w3.org/TR/
2   <html xmlns="http://www.w3.org/1999/xhtml">
3   <head>
4   <meta http-equiv="Content-Type" content="text/html; charset=UTF-8" />
5   <title>Camden Canteen</title>
6   <link href="../css/camden_canteen.css" rel="stylesheet" type="text/css" />
7   </head>
8
9   <body>
10
11  <div id="header">
12  <h1><a href="http://www.camdencanteen.com"><img src="../images/logo.png" a
        organic dining." width="230" height="224" /></a></h1>
13  </div>
14
15  <div id="navigation">
16  <ul>
17  <li><a href="http://www.camdencanteen.com" title="Camden Canteen homepa
18  <li><a href="../about/index.html" title="About the Camden Canteen">Abou
19  <li><a href="../food/index.html" title="Our restaurant and catering ser
20  <li><a href="../contact/index.html" title="Full contact details">Contac
21  </ul>
22  </div>
23
24  <div id="main">
25  <h2>Lorem ipsum dolor sit</h2>
26  <p>Lorem ipsum dolor sit amet, consectetuer adipiscing elit. Proin vel arcu
        sociosqu ad litora torquent per conubia nostra, per inceptos hymenaeos.</p>
27  <p>Morbi feugiat imperdiet neque. Nunc eget lectus eget est semper faucibus
        lobortis metus.</p>
28  <h3>Praesent id urna</h3>
29  <p>Fusce rhoncus. Fusce lobortis leo at nisl. Curabitur porttitor sem. Quis
        urna fermentum lobortis. Nunc augue. Mauris blandit ipsum et mi.</p>
30  <p>Ut facilisis, justo ac fringilla nonummy, purus eros vestibulum erat, a
        In pretium dolor et leo. In scelerisque auctor libero. Phasellus placerat tellu
31  <h4>Sed sagittis dictum nibh</h4>
```

Division tags are used to separate different areas of content. Later, they will provide useful 'hooks' for the CSS that will control their position and appearance.

one for our navigation (which will be added shortly), one for our main content (containing the remaining headings and paragraphs from our existing page), one for the related links (the left-hand column of our mock-up) and one for the page footer (which we will also add later).

Notice that the order of the various divisions in the code follows the logical structure of the document, which may not necessarily correspond to the sequence in which the same divisions appear in our final design. That is why the division that will become the column to the left of our main content – providing a space for information related to the main content – appears after the main content in the code. Note also that it is the CSS code, not the XHTML, that will control the final visual layout.

To allow us to later style them separately with CSS, each division is given a unique identifying name using the id attribute. The value you enter for each id attribute must be unique, since the aim is to identify each division individually. To deliberately style multiple elements in the same way, use the class attribute instead of id, with the same value for each element.

**must know**

Sometimes it's hard to remember which bits of code do what, or why you've even included a certain piece of code at all. To help keep track of things, add explanatory comments to your code in plain English. Comments are enclosed in < ! – – and – – >. Browsers will ignore anything that appears in-between, so the comments do not affect the actual XHTML code.

## An unordered list

What XHTML calls an unordered list is really a list of bullet points. A list can be used to represent a site's navigation device, with each individual link in the navigation being a separate item on the list. Use <ul> and </ul> tags to open and close an unordered list, and nest <li> and </li> tags inside the list for as many different items on the list

**did you know?**

Changing the `<ul>` and `</ul>` tags of an unordered list to `<ol>` and `</ol>` respectively results in an ordered or – in plain English – numbered list.

as you need. Thus the code for our site navigation so far looks like this:

```
<div id="navigation">
  <ul>
    <li>Home</li>
    <li>About us</li>
    <li>Our food</li>
    <li>Contact us</li>
  </ul>
</div>
```

### Test again

Open up your page in the browser to see the result of your code: a bulleted list. Don't worry if you do not actually want your navigation links to have bullets points next to them, and don't worry about the fact that the items are listed vertically rather than horizontally as shown on the mock-up – these are both a result of the browser's default formatting of an unordered list, which we will change later

Use the `ul` and `li` tags to create a bulleted list.

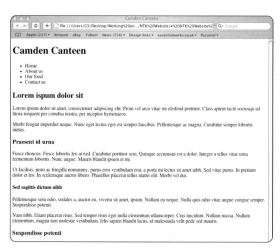

using CSS. The point is that even without CSS, our page displays in a clear and logical fashion.

**There's a humble unordered list behind the navigation of all of the above sites.**

# Adding hyperlinks

As it stands the list items are not yet links: clicking on them has no effect whatsoever. To make the text of each list item into a hyperlink, we need to add the XHTML code first shown in chapter 2.

### Links refresher

Earlier, we saw that linked text is enclosed in <a> and </a> tags and that the href attribute is added to the opening tag to tell the browser which page it should open when the link is clicked on. To make a list item a link, nest the hyperlink code for each link inside the appropriate `<li>` and `</li>` tags. Here's the code for the list item that links to our homepage:

```
<li><a
href="http://www.camdencanteen.com">Home</
a></li>
```

### Relative and absolute links

In the example above, the hyperlink code states the complete web address of the page to which the link leads. This is called an absolute link. In fact, you don't need to use an absolute link if you are linking to a page within your own site. Instead, you can use a relative link, which gives the address of the other page in relation to the current page – omitting parts of the address that are the same for both pages.

Simple in theory, this can become confusing in practice. Mistakes in this part of the code are one of the most frequent causes of 'broken links', which fail to deliver the pages they promise. No one wants a site filled with links that don't do what they say they will, so here a few examples to help you get it right:

```
<a href="contact.htm">Contact</a>
```
opens a page called 'contact.htm', so long as that page is in the same folder as the page the link is on

```
<a href="details/contact.htm">Contact</a>
```
opens 'contact.htm' when it is located within the 'details' subfolder of the folder within which both pages are located

```
<a href="../details/contact.htm">Contact</a>
```

> **must know**
>
> The file names in these examples are case sensitive, so if your file is called 'contact.htm' don't refer to it as 'Contact.htm'

opens 'contact.htm' when it is located in a folder parallel to the current folder in the site structure

In the last example, the `../` tells the browser to go one level up the folder hierarchy from the current one, before going down again into the details folder (which is therefore at the same level as the current folder). You can use as many instances of `../` as are required to get to the folder you need. For example:

`<a href="../../contact.htm">Contact</a>` looks for 'contact.htm' in a folder two levels up from the current folder

`<a href="../../details/contact.htm">Contact</a>` looks for 'contact.htm' by going two levels up from the current folder, and then one level down into a folder called 'details'.

Finally, `<a href="/contact.htm">Contact</a>` looks for 'contact.htm' in the root folder of the site (the same top level of the folder hierarchy). You can use the / to create a path from the siteroot to any area of your site – for example:

`<a href="/details/contact.htm">Contact</a>` looks for 'contact.htm' in a folder called details that is one level down from the siteroot. This is often the simplest way of managing the links on your site.

## Two additional link attributes

The href attribute is essential for a link to work, but it's not the only attribute you can add to the link element. Two particularly handy attributes are:

**must know**

Until you upload your site to your server, the h r e f attribute states a path to another file on your own computer rather than the location of another file on the web. Be careful that you don't break links by changing the location of files without updating your code. This is another reason why it's so important to plan your sitemap carefully.

# 4 Using XHTML

**did you know?**

See the W3C's list of recommended doctypes at www.w3.org/QA/2002/04/valid-dtd-list.html for more about the transitional document type declaration.

**Target** Use the target attribute with a value of _blank when you want the link to open in a new browser window. Note, however, that this attribute will not validate with a strict document type – you will need to use a 'transitional' doctype instead.

**Title** This allows you to give your link a title, which most browsers will display as a 'tooltip' – a little box of text – that appears when the cursor is moved over the link. Use this attribute to say something about the link not already stated in the link text itself, but don't make it the only way of understanding what the link does – some browsers ignore it completely.

The browser uses the value of the title attribute for the tooltip.

## Adding content to the footer and related links divisions

Finally, our mock-up had a copyright statement and some secondary navigation links at the bottom of the page. Put these in the footer division we created earlier. Note that the &copy; in the code below generates the © symbol – it's a special character which needs to be written in special XHTML code.

```
<div id="footer">
<ul>
    <li><a href="../sitemap/index.html"
title="Full list of pages on this
site">Sitemap</li></a>
    <li><a href="../accessibility.htm"
title="Our accessibility
statement">Accessibility</a></li>
</ul>
<p>&copy; Camden Canteen</p>
</div>
```

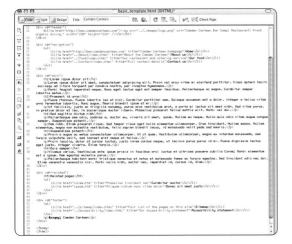

The complete page so far, with content nested in all the divisions.

In the related links division, meanwhile, add a heading and another unordered list for the links:

```
<div id="related">
<h5>Related pages</h5>
  <ul>
    <li><a href="lorem.htm"
title="Phasellus tincidunt leo">Curabitur
auctor</a></li>
    <li><a href="ipsum.htm" title="Aliquam
rutrum nunc vitae dolor">Donec sit amet
justo</a></li>
  </ul>
</div>
```

**must know**

Other special characters include curly quotation marks, ampersands and certain currency symbols. For a full list, see www.w3schools.com/tags/ref_entities.asp

# Inserting an image

So far all our content has been text, but words are only half the story. To really make your site stand out from the crowd, you will need to know how to insert pictures.

## The bigger picture

Once you've understood how hyperlinks work, it's only a short conceptual jump before you can start adding images. The key point here is that your XHTML code does not itself contain the picture, but simply tells the browser the location of a picture that should be displayed at a given point on the page. In order words, the code for an image is not dissimilar to that for a link. The code below tells the browser to display an image called logo.gif from our site's images folder:

```
<img src="../_images/logo.gif" />
```

The img tag is equivalent to the <a> and </a> tags used for a hyperlink, and the 'src' – or 'source' – attribute works in the same way as a link's href attribute. Note, however, that the img tag is entirely self-contained: instead of having an opening and closing tag, a single img tag is closed with the /> immediately proceeding its attributes – one of XHTML's small number of so-called 'self-closing' tags.

## Alt text

If the source of an image given in your XHTML is incorrect, the browser will not be able to find the image and will display a broken image icon instead.

| A non-broken image. | Broken image without alt text... | ...and one with alt text. |

Neither browsers, screen-readers or search engines can extract much useful information from this, so it's good practice to attach a brief written description to every image you use. If an image is broken, the description is displayed in its place. The browser takes the description from the `alt` attribute, which is added to the `img` tag as follows:

```
<img src="../_images/logo.gif" alt="Camden
Canteen Bar &amp; Restaurant: Fresh
organic dining." />
```

## Nesting graphics

In our file, we have already entered the title of our site as a top level heading. In our mock-up, however, the job of communicating our site's identity is done not by a textual heading but by our logo. In order to give the logo the status of our main heading, we therefore need to nest it within the `<h1>` and `</h1>` tags – replacing the existing text with the code for our logo graphic:

```
<h1><img src="../_images/logo.gif"
alt="Camden Canteen Bar &amp; Restaurant:
Fresh organic dining." /></h1>
```

**must know**

Two useful attributes associated with the `img` tag are height and width. Use them with values in pixels to tell the browser how big the image will be. The browser can then reserve this space while the image downloads. If you don't use these attributes then other elements will have to jump around to make space for images as they finish downloading – rather disconcerting for the user.

On most websites, clicking on the main logo takes the user back to the homepage. To achieve this, we need to nest the image again – this time in anchor tags (<a> and </a>) that turn the entire image into a clickable hyperlink:

```
<h1><a href="http://www.camdencanteen.com"
title="Camden Canteen homepage"><img
src="../_images/logo.gif" alt="Camden
Canteen Bar &amp; Restaurant: Fresh
organic dining." /></a></h1>
```

**The Camden Canteen logo is now the main heading, and replaces the text previously nested in the h 1 tags.**

---

**must know**

Using a graphic is the only way to reproduce a company logo on a website, but don't use graphics where a textual heading would suffice. Search engines and screen readers can only see that a graphic exists, but they can't read text embedded inside. If you must use graphical text, always give complete a l t text. Better still, investigate the CSS image-replacement techniques discussed on page 185. This provides a way of using graphical text with minimal compromise to your site's accessibility. It's a little beyond beginner level, but will soon be within your reach.

# Contact me

Whether the site you are creating is for business or pleasure, making it easy for your visitors to get in touch with you is likely to be high on your agenda.

## Reaching out to your public

Keen to encourage customers to refer to online information, many businesses bury their telephone numbers and address details deep within their sites. Exactly how much information you choose to give away will depend on your individual circumstances, but allowing users to email you is a bare minimum.

## Email links

Email links are an easy way to receive email via your website. They look like ordinary links, and the XHTML behind them is based on the same anchor tags used to link to another web page. But when a user clicks on an email link, their email application opens with a new blank email addressed to you.

**Not all websites make it as straightforward as CNN.com to contact the site's authors.**

### Security

Unfortunately, any email addresses included in your XHTML document are vulnerable to malicious 'spammers', who can use them to send junk messages in your name. To prevent this, it is a good idea to encyrpt any email addresses in your code. Download a free program such as MailTo-Encryptor (Windows) and MailtoEncoder (Mac) to generate encrypted versions of email addresses and use them to replace the original addresses in your code.

**watch out!**
Think carefully before publishing any personal information online. Once online, personal telephone numbers and email addresses can soon find their way onto search engines like Google. If you are publishing other people's details, get their permission first.

## Adding a Mailto link

```
    Curabitur semper lobortis metus.</p>
30      <h3>Praesent id urna</h3>
31      <p>Fusce rhoncus. Fusce lobortis leo at nisl. Curabitur por
    Integer a tellus vitae urna fermentum lobortis. Nunc augue. Mauris
32      <p>Ut facilisis, justo ac fringilla nonummy, purus eros ves
    nibh. Sed vitae purus. In pretium dolor et leo. In scelerisque auct
    elit. Morbi vel dui.</p>
33      <h4>Sed sagittis dictum nibh</h4>
34      <p>Pellentesque sem odio, sodales a, auctor eu, viverra sit
    odio vitae augue congue semper. Suspendisse potenti.</p>
35      <p>Nam nibh. Etiam placerat risus. Sed tempor risus eget nu
    Nullam massa. Nullam elementum, magna non molestie vestibulum, feli
    pede sed mauris.</p>
36      <h3>Suspendisse potenti</h3>
37      <p>Proin a augue ac metus consectetuer ullamcorper. Ut ut q
    interdum malesuada, sem turpis vulputate velit, sed laoreet erat ne
38      <p>Proin iaculis, dolor at cursus luctus, justo lorem cursu
    dignissim lectus eget justo. Integer viverra. Etiam turpis.</p>
39      <h4>Duis semper</h4>
40      <p>Vivamus varius. Vestibulum ante ipsum primis in faucibus
    Curae; Morbi elementum est a ipsum. Nam egestas molestie purus.</p>
41      <p>Pellentesque habitant morbi tristique senectus et netus
    tincidunt odio nec dui. Etiam venenatis venenatis nisi. Morbi nulla
    diam.</p>
42      <p><a></a></p>
43      </div>
44
45      <div id="related">
46      <h5>Related pages</h5>
47      <ul>
48      <li><a href="lorem.htm" title="Phasellus tincidunt leo"
49      <li><a href="ipsum.htm" title="Aliquam rutrum nunc vita
50      </ul>
51      </div>
```

```
    Curabitur semper lobortis metus.</p>
30      <h3>Praesent id urna</h3>
31      <p>Fusce rhoncus. Fusce lobortis leo at nisl. Curabitur por
    Integer a tellus vitae urna fermentum lobortis. Nunc augue. Mauris
32      <p>Ut facilisis, justo ac fringilla nonummy, purus eros ves
    nibh. Sed vitae purus. In pretium dolor et leo. In scelerisque auct
    elit. Morbi vel dui.</p>
33      <h4>Sed sagittis dictum nibh</h4>
34      <p>Pellentesque sem odio, sodales a, auctor eu, viverra sit
    odio vitae augue congue semper. Suspendisse potenti.</p>
35      <p>Nam nibh. Etiam placerat risus. Sed tempor risus eget nu
    Nullam massa. Nullam elementum, magna non molestie vestibulum, feli
    pede sed mauris.</p>
36      <h3>Suspendisse potenti</h3>
37      <p>Proin a augue ac metus consectetuer ullamcorper. Ut ut q
    interdum malesuada, sem turpis vulputate velit, sed laoreet erat ne
38      <p>Proin iaculis, dolor at cursus luctus, justo lorem cursu
    dignissim lectus eget justo. Integer viverra. Etiam turpis.</p>
39      <h4>Duis semper</h4>
40      <p>Vivamus varius. Vestibulum ante ipsum primis in faucibus
    Curae; Morbi elementum est a ipsum. Nam egestas molestie purus.</p>
41      <p>Pellentesque habitant morbi tristique senectus et netus
    tincidunt odio nec dui. Etiam venenatis venenatis nisi. Morbi nulla
    diam.</p>
42      <p><a>Email us!</a></p>
43      </div>
44
45      <div id="related">
46      <h5>Related pages</h5>
47      <ul>
48      <li><a href="lorem.htm" title="Phasellus tincidunt leo"
49      <li><a href="ipsum.htm" title="Aliquam rutrum nunc vita
50      </ul>
51      </div>
```

**1** Open your XHTML document and go to the point where you would like to add an email link. Add **<a>** and **</a>** tags as if you were creating a normal link.

**2** In-between the two anchor tags, enter the content that users will click on in order to start their email. This example shows a text link, but you can also use an image.

```
    Curabitur semper lobortis metus.</p>
30      <h3>Praesent id urna</h3>
31      <p>Fusce rhoncus. Fusce lobortis leo at nisl. Curabitur por
    Integer a tellus vitae urna fermentum lobortis. Nunc augue. Mauris
32      <p>Ut facilisis, justo ac fringilla nonummy, purus eros vest
    nibh. Sed vitae purus. In pretium dolor et leo. In scelerisque auct
    elit. Morbi vel dui.</p>
33      <h4>Sed sagittis dictum nibh</h4>
34      <p>Pellentesque sem odio, sodales a, auctor eu, viverra sit
    odio vitae augue congue semper. Suspendisse potenti.</p>
35      <p>Nam nibh. Etiam placerat risus. Sed tempor risus eget nu
    Nullam massa. Nullam elementum, magna non molestie vestibulum, feli
    pede sed mauris.</p>
36      <h3>Suspendisse potenti</h3>
37      <p>Proin a augue ac metus consectetuer ullamcorper. Ut ut q
    interdum malesuada, sem turpis vulputate velit, sed laoreet erat ne
38      <p>Proin iaculis, dolor at cursus luctus, justo lorem cursu
    dignissim lectus eget justo. Integer viverra. Etiam turpis.</p>
39      <h4>Duis semper</h4>
40      <p>Vivamus varius. Vestibulum ante ipsum primis in faucibus
    Curae; Morbi elementum est a ipsum. Nam egestas molestie purus.</p>
41      <p>Pellentesque habitant morbi tristique senectus et netus
    tincidunt odio nec dui. Etiam venenatis venenatis nisi. Morbi nulla
    diam.</p>
42      <p><a href="mailto:info@camdencanteen.com">Email us!</a></p
43      </div>
44
45      <div id="related">
46      <h5>Related pages</h5>
47      <ul>
48      <li><a href="lorem.htm" title="Phasellus tincidunt leo">
49      <li><a href="ipsum.htm" title="Aliquam rutrum nunc vita
50      </ul>
51      </div>
```

**3** Add the **href** attribute to the opening anchor tag. Its value should be `mailto` followed by a colon and then the email address to which the message will be sent. In our example, the complete code for the link is: `<a href="mailto:info@camdencanteen.com">Email us!</a>`

**4** Save the XHTML document and open it in a web browser. When you click on the email link, your email application opens with a new message addressed to the email address you entered.

# Tables

It is hard to beat the convenience and clarity of tabular data. Use XHTML tables to structure content such as timetables, pricelists and side-by-side product comparisons.

## Anatomy of a table

Tables are composed of individual nuggets of data arranged in rows and columns. Each piece of information has its own cell in the table, with each row or column serving to group cells that are common to a particular item or category. This familiar structure is easily translated into XHTML code, and the opening times of Camden Canteen are typical of the information that should be structured in this way.

### Creating a table in XHTML

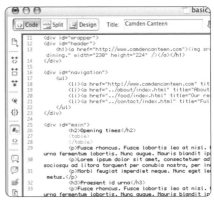

**1** Start by working out how many rows and columns you will need. Sketch out your table on a piece of paper, or use a spreadsheet. This table of opening times has three columns (one for the day of the week, one for the opening time and one for the closing time) and eight rows (one for each day of the week, plus a heading row to label each column).

**2** Open your XHTML document and place the cursor at the point in the body of the document where the table is to appear. On a new line of code, type `<table>` to mark the start of a table. Afterwards, close the table element with `</table>`. The cells, rows and columns of your table will all be nested between these two tags.

```
16  <div id="navigation">
17    <ul>
18      <li><a href="http://www.camdencanteen.com" tit
19      <li><a href="../about/index.html" title="About
20      <li><a href="../food/index.html" title="Our res
21      <li><a href="../contact/index.html" title="Ful
22    </ul>
23  </div>
24
25  <div id="main">
26    <h2>Opening times</h2>
27    <table>
28      <tr></tr>
29      <tr></tr>
30      <tr></tr>
31      <tr></tr>
32      <tr></tr>
33      <tr></tr>
34      <tr></tr>
35      <tr></tr>
36    </table>
37    <p>Fusce rhoncus. Fusce lobortis leo at nisl. C
   urna fermentum lobortis. Nunc augue. Mauris blandit ips
38    <p>Lorem ipsum dolor sit amet, consectetuer adi
   sociosqu ad litora torquent per conubia nostra, per ind
39    <p>Morbi feugiat imperdiet neque. Nunc eget led
   metus.</p>
40    <h3>Praesent id urna</h3>
41    <p>Fusce rhoncus. Fusce lobortis leo at nisl. C
   urna fermentum lobortis. Nunc augue. Mauris blandit ips
42    <p>Ut facilisis, justo ac fringilla nonummy, pu
   pretium dolor et leo. In scelerisque auctor libero. Ph
43    <h4>Sed sagittis dictum nibh</h4>
44    <p>Pellentesque sem odio, sodales a, auctor eu
```

```
16  <div id="navigation">
17    <ul>
18      <li><a href="http://www.camdencanteen.com" tit
19      <li><a href="../about/index.html" title="About
20      <li><a href="../food/index.html" title="Our res
21      <li><a href="../contact/index.html" title="Ful
22    </ul>
23  </div>
24
25  <div id="main">
26    <h2>Opening times</h2>
27    <table>
28      <tr>
29        <th>Day</th>
30        <th>Opening time</th>
31        <th>Closing time</th>
32      </tr>
33      <tr></tr>
34      <tr></tr>
35      <tr></tr>
36      <tr></tr>
37      <tr></tr>
38      <tr></tr>
39      <tr></tr>
40    </table>
41    <p>Fusce rhoncus. Fusce lobortis leo at nisl. C
   urna fermentum lobortis. Nunc augue. Mauris blandit ips
42    <p>Lorem ipsum dolor sit amet, consectetuer adi
   sociosqu ad litora torquent per conubia nostra, per ind
43    <p>Morbi feugiat imperdiet neque. Nunc eget led
   metus.</p>
44    <h3>Praesent id urna</h3>
45    <p>Fusce rhoncus. Fusce lobortis leo at nisl. C
   urna fermentum lobortis. Nunc augue. Mauris blandit ip
```

**3** The table row tags `<tr>` and `</tr>` are used to create each row of the table. We need eight rows, so enter eight pairs of these tags. To keep things tidy, indent each row on a new line of code.

**4** The first row of the table will consist of the heading of each column. Use the `<th>` tag to open the table heading of the first column, enter the column name (in this case, it's the day of the week) and then close the heading with the `</th>` tag. Repeat for each heading, so that all three column headings are nested within the first table row.

```
16  <div id="navigation">
17    <ul>
18      <li><a href="http://www.camdencanteen.com" tit
19      <li><a href="../about/index.html" title="About
20      <li><a href="../food/index.html" title="Our res
21      <li><a href="../contact/index.html" title="Ful
22    </ul>
23  </div>
24
25  <div id="main">
26    <h2>Opening times</h2>
27    <table>
28      <tr>
29        <th>Day</th>
30        <th>Opening time</th>
31        <th>Closing time</th>
32      </tr>
33      <tr>
34        <td>Monday</td>
35        <td>12.00</td>
36        <td>23.00</td>
37      </tr>
38      <tr></tr>
39      <tr></tr>
40      <tr></tr>
41      <tr></tr>
42      <tr></tr>
43      <tr></tr>
44    </table>
45    <p>Fusce rhoncus. Fusce lobortis leo at nisl. C
   urna fermentum lobortis. Nunc augue. Mauris blandit ips
46    <p>Lorem ipsum dolor sit amet, consectetuer adi
   sociosqu ad litora torquent per conubia nostra, per ind
47    <p>Morbi feugiat imperdiet neque. Nunc eget le
```

```
25  <div id="main">
26    <h2>Opening times</h2>
27    <table>
28      <tr>
29        <th>Day</th>
30        <th>Opening time</th>
31        <th>Closing time</th>
32      </tr>
33      <tr>
34        <td>Monday</td>
35        <td>12.00</td>
36        <td>23.00</td>
37      </tr>
38      <tr>
39        <td>Tuesday</td>
40        <td>12.00</td>
41        <td>23.00</td>
42      </tr>
43      <tr>
44        <td>Wednesday</td>
45        <td>12.00</td>
46        <td>17.00</td>
47      </tr>
48      <tr>
49        <td>Thursday</td>
50        <td>12.00</td>
51        <td>23.00</td>
52      </tr>
53      <tr>
54        <td>Friday</td>
55        <td>12.00</td>
56        <td>1.00</td>
57      </tr>
58      <tr>
59        <td>Saturday</td>
60        <td>9.30</td>
61        <td>1.00</td>
62      </tr>
63      <tr>
64        <td>Sunday</td>
65        <td>11.30</td>
66        <td>15.30</td>
67      </tr>
68    </table>
69    <p>Fusce rhoncus. Fusce lobortis leo at nisl. Curabitur porttitor sem. C
   urna fermentum lobortis. Nunc augue. Mauris blandit ipsum at mi.</p>
70    <p>Lorem ipsum dolor sit amet, consectetuer adipiscing elit. Proin ned
```

**5** Now move to the next row of the table, which in this example shows the restaurant opening times on Monday. There will be three cells in this row: one for the day, one for the opening time and one for the closing time. Type `<td>` to open the first cell, then enter the cell's content (here, 'Monday') and then close the cell with a `</td>` tag. Repeat for the other two cells.

**6** Complete the table by nesting three pairs of `<td>` and `</td>` tags within each of the remaining rows. As before, enter the content of each cell within its `<td>` and `</td>` tags.

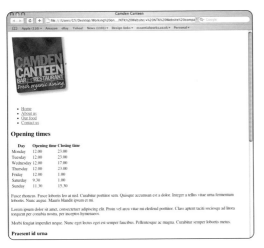

7 Save your XHTML document and open it in a browser to see the finished table. The structure should match your initial sketch. Don't worry about the formatting of your table – you can use CSS to change its colours, dimensions and typography later.

Tables were once used to create complete layouts, using different cells for headers, columns and footers. Since the technique mixes content and presentation, it is no longer considered good practice. Use tables for tabular data only, and leave layout and styling to the CSS techniques covered in the next chapter.

**did you know?**

Using XHTML tables is the best way to publish tabular data on your site. However, if you want users to be able to download data such as Excel, upload the document to your server and use the anchor tags shown on page 23 to create a link to it. When the link is clicked, the file is downloaded.

**want to know more?**

• For a more detailed discussion of different doctypes, see the W3C recommendations at www.w3.org/QA/2002/04/valid-dtd-list.html

• Definition lists (nested in < d l > and < / d l > tags) are another type of XHTML list, used to list terms (nested in < d t > and < d t > tags) with their definitions (nested in < d d > and < d d > tags).

• As your web skills improve, consider replacing email links with online forms. Developing a form combines XHTML code – for items such as checkboxes and drop-down menus – with programming that processes the form and sends its contents to a database or email address. There's a good introduction at www.webstartcenter.com/howto/forms.php

# 5 Using CSS

You should now be able to present content in a well-structured, standards-compliant XHTML web page. However, the visual impact of pure XHTML is rather underwhelming. To recreate the mock-up, we'll need to call upon the power of Cascading Style Sheets (CSS) to style our XHTML and make our website stand out from the crowd. This chapter is a toolbox of practical CSS techniques. Get them under your belt and you will really be able to unleash your creativity.

# Creating a Cascading Style Sheet

Cascading style sheets are straightforward documents and you should have no problem creating successful ones. It's simply a question of understanding the rules behind them.

## CSS refresher

You saw in the previous chapter that a Cascading Style Sheet is used to control the layout and formatting of the content contained in an XHTML file. Just as with XHTML files, CSS files are simply coded text, which you can write in a simple text or code editor. Alternatively, WYSIWYG editors can write CSS code for you, based on the formatting options you specify.

## Anatomy of a CSS file

CSS files are simpler in structure than XHTML files. There are no document type, head or body tags to worry about – just a series of rules applied to different elements of XHTML. You can write the rules in any order you like, since the order in which they will be applied is determined by the hierarchy of the cascade.

## Creating and linking a CSS file

It is possible to write CSS rules directly within an XHTML document, but it is almost always preferable to keep the CSS rules in a separate CSS file. This way, you are able to apply blanket changes to the formatting of your entire site with only one change to the style sheet.

Keeping all your CSS code in a separate document also maintains the strict division of content (in the

**must know**

Skip back to page 28 to see how CSS rules are composed and applied to XHTML.

In fact, the flexible structure of CSS files does not always make them easy to work with. As your site gets more complicated, your style sheet can easily become unwieldy. That's why it's particularly useful to explain your CSS rules with comments. The principle of CSS comments is the same as for XHTML comments, but in a CSS file a comment is opened with /* and closed with */

Without the style sheet, this page loses all its formatting – but its well-structured XHTML ensures that the content still makes sense.

XHTML document) and presentation. The separation of content and its presentation is always desirable, since it allows you to reformat the same material in different ways for different purposes. For example, many designers use this technique to adapt the presentation of a site's content for mobile devices or printers. Layouts can be modified to fit on smaller screens, and elements that are only useful on screen – such as navigation devices – can be hidden for the printed page. Style sheets used in this way can also boost accessibility. You could, for example, use different style sheets to provide an alternative high-contrast colour scheme for your site.

## Creating and linking a CSS file

**1** Start a new blank document in your text or code editor and save it in the _css folder created for it earlier. Remember that the style sheet must be saved with a .css file extension for the browser to recognize it as a CSS document.

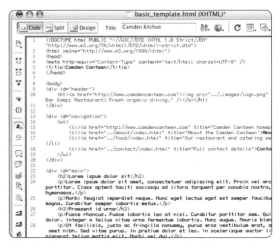

**2** To link the new style sheet to the content it will format, return to your XHTML document and locate the *head* element of the code.

**3** Nest a new self-closing element called `link` inside the `head` element.

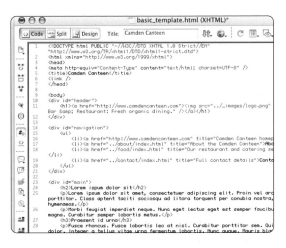

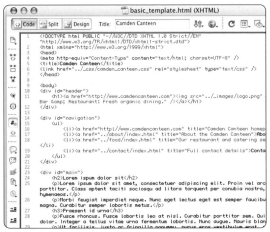

**4** The `link` element tells the browser about your style sheet. Include the `rel` and type attributes as shown, and change the value of the `href` attribute to match the file name and location of the style sheet you are linking to (in this example, the style sheet was saved as `camden_canteen.css` and is located in the `_css` folder).

```
<head>
  <title>Camden Canteen</title>
  <link href="../_css/style.css" rel="style
sheet" type="text/css" />
</head>
```

**must know**

Note that the `href` attribute here works just as does the same attribute in an anchor tag. If the link is wrong, the browser will not be able to find the style sheet and will display your XHTML using its own default formatting. Because the XHTML is well structured, the page still makes sense even without the CSS.

# A splash of colour

With the style sheet linked, you can finally get a bit more creative. Choosing your own colours for the page background and text is not only a way of branding your site, but also a means of improving its usability.

## Colour on the web

**Modern computer monitors can display millions of colours.**

Computer monitors display colour by mixing different shades of red, green and blue light. There are 256 shades of each of these core colours, so multiplying 256 x 256 x 256 gives a total of 16,777,216 colours to choose from. Unfortunately, things are not quite this simple. Though most computer screens in use today are capable of producing all 16.7 million combinations of red, green and blue, a small minority of users still use monitors that display a much smaller range of colours. That's where web-safe colours come in.

### The web-safe colour palette

The most basic colour screens can display 256 colours. Although this figure is the same for both Windows and Apple Macintosh computers, only 216 of these colours are common to both operating systems, and it is these 216 colours that make up the web-safe colour palette.

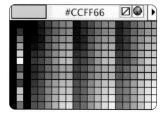

**The 216 colours that make up the web-safe colour palette.**

Web-safe colours can be relied upon to display smoothly, even on the oldest machines. By contrast, when an old monitor encounters a non-web safe colour it attempts to replicate it using a pattern of coloured pixels it can display. This process is known as dithering, and the results are often far

from satisfactory. In the very worst case, dithered colours can render a page practically illegible.

**The second image has been reduced to the 216 web-safe colours, causing visible dithering.**

## Safety first?

The big problem with the web-safe palette is that 216 colours are not really enough. The range of hues on offer isn't very well balanced, and it's certainly far too narrow to produce a smooth and realistic transition of colours in a photograph. Since some 80 per cent of users now use monitors that can produce a full range of colours, it's tempting to consign the web-safe palette to history. That said, a truly accessible site shouldn't ignore users of older screens, and it's worth remembering that even relatively new mobile devices may still have pretty basic colour displays.

With this in mind, it's probably best to stick to web-safe colours for text and page backgrounds, while using a wider range of colours for photographs and graphics that will not impede your site's usability if not displayed exactly as you intended.

**did you know?**
You will find regularly updated statistics on users' screen specifications on the W3C website at www.w3schools.com/browsers/browsers_display.asp

## Choosing colours

You can specify colours in your CSS rules in the following three ways:

**By name** Sixteen basic colours can be specified. This is easy to understand, but you will soon tire of aqua, black, blue, fuchsia, gray, green, lime, maroon, navy, olive, purple, red, silver, teal, white, and yellow.

**By RGB value** Setting colours by using the 256 shades of red, green and blue allows you to access all 16,777,216 colours.

**By hexadecimal value** Hexadecimal (hex) values are another way of naming RGB values using a six-character code of letters and numbers. Hex codes are not as complicated as they look, and can often be written in a three-character shorthand format.

**Different rules, same result:**

**Name or RGB value:**

```
body {
    color: rgb(255,255,0);
    background-color: red;
}
```

**Hex values (long- and shorthand):**

```
body {
    color: #FFFF00;
    background-color: #F00;
}
```

### Lorem ispum dolor sit

Morbi feugiat imperdiet neque. Nunc eget lectus eget est semper faucibus. Pellentesque ac magna. Curabitur semper lobortis metus. Fusce rhoncus. Fusce lobortis leo at nisl. Curabitur porttitor sem. Quisque accumsan est a dolor. Integer a tellus vitae urna fermentum lobortis. Nunc augue. Mauris blandit ipsum et mi.

Ut facilisis, justo ac fringilla nonummy, purus eros vestibulum erat, a porta mi lectus sit amet nibh. Sed vitae purus. In pretium dolor et leo. In scelerisque auctor libero. Phasellus placerat tellus mattis elit. Morbi vel dui.

### Pellentesque sem odio

Sodales a, auctor eu, viverra sit amet, ipsum. Nullam eu neque. Nulla quis odio vitae augue congue semper. Suspendisse potenti. Nam nibh. Etiam placerat risus. Sed tempor risus eget nulla elementum ullamcorper. Cras tincidunt. Nullam massa. Nullam elementum, magna non molestie vestibulum, felis sapien blandit lacus, id malesuada velit pede sed mauris.

## Colour coded

Whether you choose to use RGB or hex values, you will need to work out the correct values for your chosen colour. The easiest way to do this is by using the colour picker in your graphics application. The steps below show the Photoshop colour picker, but other applications work in a similar way.

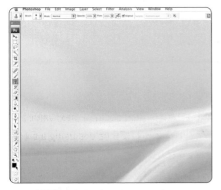

1 Open your graphics application and bring up the colour picker. In Photoshop, this is done by double-clicking the current colour swatch in the toolbar.

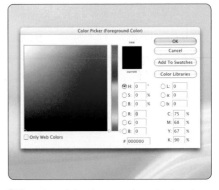

2 The colour picker shows a colour wheel on the left, with values for the current colour on the right. Note the RGB and hex (shown as #) values.

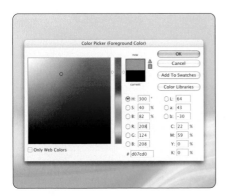

3 Move the slider up and down to change the colours shown in the large square on the left. Click anywhere on the square to pick a colour. Make a note of its RGB or hex value to use in your CSS rule.

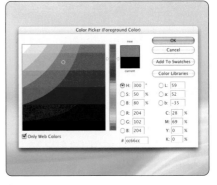

4 To restrict the choice of colours to web-safe colours only, click the 'Only Web Colors' checkbox. If the colour isn't web safe, its values will 'snap' automatically to the nearest web-safe colour.

The light grey text in the top example may be difficult for some users to read easily.

**must know**

If you are creating a corporate website for a company that already has an established visual identity, use this to inform your choice of colours. If you are starting from scratch, get some inspiration from colour-scheme websites such as www.kuler.adobe.com, http://wellstyled.com/tools/colorscheme2, www.colorblender.com and http://netcocktail.com

## Compare and contrast

While the web-safe palette will always produce solid colours on screen, the exact colour you see will vary depending on the individual user's monitor, and their individual brightness and contrast settings. Bear in mind, too, that text can become difficult to read if the foreground colour doesn't contrast sufficiently with the background colour. To avoid this problem, check your chosen colour using an online colour analysis tool (such as at http://snook.ca/technical/colour_contrast/colour.html). This checks the contrast between your foreground and background colour against the W3C's accessibility guidelines.

You might also wish to see your site design through the eyes of someone who is colour blind. The Vischeck website (www.vischeck.com) lets you see how individual images and even entire web pages appear to users with three different types of colour blindness. If the results render your pages unusable you will be well advised to rethink your colour choices.

# Colour me beautiful

Once you've selected the colours that you wish to use for your site, you will need to create CSS rules in your style sheet that apply those colours to specific XHTML elements.

**Adding colours to the body element**

Since many colour choices apply to the entire web page, they can be specified in a rule that targets the body element of your XHTML code. Our mock-up used black text on a cream background. To achieve this with CSS, use the color and background-color properties respectively:

```
body {
    color: #000000;
    background-color: #FFFFCC;
}
```

This rule uses hex values to specify two contrasting web-safe colours. Note the hash (#) symbol before the colour references. These colour values are composed of three pairs of two characters. Where both characters in each pair are the same – as they are with all web-safe colours – the colour values can be written in a leaner, shorthand format. The final rule is:

```
body {
    color: #000;
    background-color: #FFC;
}
```

**must know**

If you're using a Mac, you will not find a hash key on your keyboard. Instead, hold down the ALT key and press 3 at the top of the keyboard (not the 3 key in the numeric section of the keyboard). Alternatively, show the character palette and double click on the hash symbol.

## Testing times

To see your XHTML and CSS files in action, save both files and open the XHTML template in your browser. If the colours are not the ones you expected, check that the style sheet is linked to the XHTML document correctly. You should also check your CSS code at regular intervals, using the W3C CSS Validation Service at http://jigsaw.w3.org/css-validator. It works in just the same way as the XHTML validator.

**With the XHTML document and CSS style sheet linked, we can start to style content.**

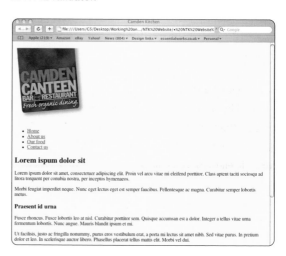

## Colouring headings

Our text is now coloured black, but the second level headings on our mock-up were in fact dark green. To override the colour set for the body element, choose a colour for the dark green and create a new rule using XHTML's h2 element as a selector:

```
h2 {
    color: #363;
}
```

In this screen the headings have been changed to dark green as in our mock-up.

You might want all the headings – not just the second level headings – to be the same colour. Rather than create a separate rule for each heading, you can apply the same property to a series of XHTML elements as follows:

```
h1, h2, h3, h4, h5, h6 {
    color: #363;
}
```

## Styling links

By default, most browsers colour links blue when first displayed, red when clicked upon (when 'active') and dark blue when the user has already visited them. If this clashes with your own colour scheme, restyle the different states of links with CSS. In our case, the mock-up calls for different shades of green for links, active links and visited links. We will also change the link colour when the user holds the mouse – or hovers – over a link.

**try this**

This technique is not restricted to changing text colours. You will use the same approach to achieve much more sophisticated designs, using the full range of CSS properties. If you are impatient to experiment, try setting the background-color property for a heading element.

## Using pseudo-classes

A simple rule to target and set a text colour for all the anchor (hyperlink) elements in our XHTML can be written just like the rule that restyled the headings:

```
a {
    color: #393;
}
```

This is fine, but there's no reference to the state of the link. Pseudo-classes provide this, adding a new bit of code to the anchor selector. The basic rule becomes:

```
a:link {
    color: #393;
}
```

Further rules with pseudo-classes are then used to style the other link states:

```
a:visited {
    color: #363;
}
```

**Using pseudo-classes: these links are different shades of green in link and visited states.**

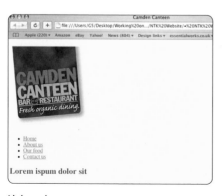

**Link mode**

**Visited mode**

**Hovering mode**

**Active mode**

```
a:hover {
  color: #6C6;
}
```

This time the links are different shades of green for the hover and active states.

```
a:active {
  color: #3C6;
}
```

## The underlining issue

Unless instructed otherwise, browsers will always underline hyperlinked text. Underlining is not the only way to identify links, and there may be occasions where the underline gets in the way. If so, use CSS's text-decoration property with a value of none to remove it. For example, the rule below makes the text of a link white on a black background when the user hovers over it, removing the underline in the process:

```
a:hover {
  color: #FFF;
  background-color: #000;
  text-decoration: none;
}
```

**did you know?**

Underlining is a widely understood convention, so think carefully before removing underlines, as doing so may make your site less user-friendly. Underlining is a good way of signalling a link to those who may not be able to distinguish links from surrounding text by colour alone.

# Typography on the web

CSS has given web designers a level of typographic control once reserved for printed documents, and overriding the browser's default font choices goes a long way towards establishing your site's unique character. Unfortunately, there are still some major limitations you will have to work around.

## Hobson's choice

When you type a letter or work with a designer to create a corporate brochure, you can print your work using any font you like. In web design, you can ask the browser to display your page in a particular font, but it will only be able to honour your request if the font you specify is already installed on the user's computer. If it isn't, the browser will have to use a different font instead.

There's little point specifying fonts which most users are unlikely to have, so the safest option is to stick to fonts which are already installed on most computers before they are sold. These are often referred to as 'browser-safe fonts', and there's a grand total of just three truly browser-safe fonts to choose from.

**did you know?**

Serif fonts such as Times New Roman have little 'feet' at the end of each character stroke. Sans-serif fonts such as Arial do not. Serif fonts are often said to be more legible in print, but the same is not necessarily true on screen.

## Three core fonts

You will find these fonts on almost every personal computer on the planet.

These words are set in Times New Roman, *Times Italic* and **Times Bold**.

**Times New Roman** This ubiquitous serif typeface, originally designed for *The Times* newspaper, is a very safe bet indeed. Most browsers use it as their default font.

**Arial** This is the most commonly installed sans-serif font. It's often used as an alternative to the iconic Helvetica, although closer inspection reveals significant differences between the two.

These words are set in Arial, *Arial Italic* and **Arial Bold**.

**Courier New** This is a monospaced font, meaning that each letter occupies the same amount of horizontal space on the page, a bit like an old-fashioned typewriter. It's generally used for quoting snippets of code.

```
These words are
set in Courier New,
Courier Italic
and Courier Bold.
```

### Two extra fonts

Georgia and Verdana were both freely distributed by Microsoft. Although not quite as prevalent as the typefaces listed above, they can still be found on most modern computers. The proportions of both were specially designed to make these typefaces legible on screen, so making them especially interesting for web designers.

**Georgia** is a quirky serif font that makes an interesting alternative to Times New Roman.

These words are set in Georgia, *Georgia Italic* and **Georgia Bold**.

**Verdana** is a sans-serif font in the humanist tradition, reminiscent of classic typefaces like Frutiger and Gill Sans.

These words are set in Verdana, *Verdana Italic* and **Verdana Bold**.

**did you know?**

There's a useful list of fonts distributed with various Windows and Macintosh software (see www.microsoft.com/typography/fonts/default.aspx). See also the font statistics at www.codestyle.org

# Specifying fonts in CSS

Since you can never really be sure which fonts your site's visitors will have installed, CSS allows you to specify a list of fonts in order of preference. You can list as many fonts as you like, followed – as a last resort – by a generic term such as serif or sans-serif. Font choices are specified as values of CSS's font-family property. In the rule below, this property is set for the body element of our XHTML, meaning that it will affect all text within the <body> and </body> tags. Note that font names consisting of more than one word, such as Times New Roman below, must be enclosed in double quote marks.

```
body {
    font-family: Georgia, "Times New Roman",
    serif;
}
```

**The main text on the page below is set in Georgia. If the user does not have Georgia installed, the text is displayed in Times New Roman instead.**

Now any text within the body of your XHTML page will be set in Georgia if it is available, if not Times New Roman will be selected. If neither Georgia nor

Times New Roman are installed, the browser will choose a serif font that is. Note that each choice is separated by a comma.

## Font size and leading

In printed documents, font sizes and leading – the amount of space between each line of text – are specified in absolute units such as points. You can specify absolute font sizes in CSS rules, too, but a more accessible approach is to use relative units. This ensures that users will be able to enlarge the text on your site if they are unable to read it at the original size, while maintaining the relationship between the different sizes of paragraph and heading text.

**Three relative units**

There are three different ways of specifying relative font sizes in CSS:

**Written values** Based around a default value of medium, you can set text to be xx-small, x-small, small, large, x-large or xx-large. You can also choose smaller or larger, which decrease or increase the size of the text selected by a CSS rule in relation to the text-size of the XHTML element above it. For example, you could set anchor text to be smaller than the paragraph text within which it sits. This system is simple to understand, but bear in mind that the range of sizes available to you is limited.

**Percentage** Assuming that 100 per cent is the size at which a browser displays text by default, you can

**must know**
There are five generic font family values: serif, sans-serif, cursive, monospace and fantasy. Cursive and fantasy are used to specify highly decorative scripts. However, a browser will classify a whole range of varied fonts as 'fantasy', so specifying this category may in fact give you little control over the appearance of your text.

set percentage values for all the different text styles on your web page as a percentage of this default size.

**Ems** In traditional typography, one em was the horizontal width of the uppercase M. In CSS, the width of an em applied to an XHTML element is derived from the size of type specified for its parent element. Hence a rule declaring that the font size of top level headings (h1) should be 2em results in text that is twice the size of the text size specified for the body element, since this is the parent of the h1 element. Ems are the unit of measurement recommended by the W3C.

**CSS rules for font size and leading**

Type size and leading are set using the `font-size` and `line-height` properties respectively. The rule below, for example, sets the size and line-height of all text enclosed in XHTML paragraph tags:

```
p {
    font-size: 1.2em;
    line-height: 1.5em;
}
```

## Bold and italic fonts

You can use the `font-style` property with a value of `italic` to italicize whole elements of text, and the `font-weight` property with a value of `bold` to embolden them. To get the bold headings shown in our mock-up, for example, we could expand the existing heading rule as follows:

**did you know?**
Increasing the default line-height can improve the legibility of paragraph text on screen.

```
h1, h2, h3, h4, h5, h6 {
  color: #609;
  font-weight: bold;
}
```

Note, however, that you'll need to edit your XHTML to italicize or embolden specific words or phrases within a block of text. Adding additional XHTML to format text instead of formatting existing XHTML using CSS rules appears to compromise the strict separation of content and presentation, but this need not necessarily be the case. Emphasizing certain words is as much a grammatical issue as it is a presentational one, and including italics within the XHTML document ensures grammatical correctness is maintained regardless of any purely presentational styling. In the paragraph below, <em> and </em> tags – meaning emphasis, and not to be confused with the em measurement – are added around the foreign words that should be displayed in italics:

```
<p>Faced with the task of creating a
website, initial <em>Angst</em> gave way to
a certain <em>savoir faire</em>.</p>
```

For bold text, replace the <em> and </em> tags with <strong> and </strong> respectively.

## Small capitals
Used with restraint, smalls caps can be an elegant way to style text. To produce small caps with CSS, use the font-variant property with a value of small-caps.

**alistapart.com is not only an incredible resource of articles on web design, it's also a prime example of fine web typography.**

## Transforming text

The rather dramatic-sounding `text-transform` property is used to control the case of text. The most useful values are `capitalize`, `lowercase` and `uppercase`.

This is a particularly good example of how CSS can format large amounts of content quickly without undermining the integrity of the original data. Take the example of a modern design which – throwing good grammar out of the window – calls for all headings to be written in lowercase text. We could simply enter lowercase headings into our XHTML document, but this would mean introducing deliberate mistakes into what should be pure content, and if lowercase headings were ever to fall out of favour we'd have to manually retype every last heading on the entire website. A much better approach is to specify the `text-transform` property in a rule for headings:

```
h1, h2, h3, h4, h5, h6 {
    text-transform: lowercase;
}
```

If the use of correct English grammar becomes more popular, we can change all the lowercase headings with just one quick edit to the style sheet.

## Text alignment

The `text-align` property in CSS makes it easy to align text with a value of `left`, `right` or `center`. You can also set a value of `justify`, although beware that this can create very unsightly gaps between words – especially when text is enlarged.

**must know**

Print designers are used to fine-tuning the flow of text by inserting manual line breaks at the ends of lines that appear to stick out further than those around them. Web designers do not – yet – have this luxury: the flow of lines will change according to whether the user resizes the text and – in a fluid design – the size of the user's screen.

# Font shorthand

The rule below uses the font properties we've described so far to style a second level heading:

```
h2 {
    font-style: italic;
    font-variant: small-caps;
    font-weight: bold;
    font-size: 1.2em;
    line-height: 1.5em;
    font-family: Georgia, "Times New Roman",
    serif;
}
```

Looking at this one rule alone, it's easy to see how style sheets can easily become rather cumbersome documents. The CSS font property is useful because it can simplify things a little by combining all the settings above in one line of code, with each value separated by a space:

```
h2 {
    font: italic small-caps bold 1.2em/1.5em
    Georgia, "Times New Roman", serif;
}
```

The order of the values here is font-style, font-variant, font-weight, font-size, line-height and font-family. Not all the values need to be listed, but those that are must be written in this order if they are to work correctly. Note that the values for font-size and line-height are given as one value, with the font-size and line-height separated by a forward slash.

**must know**

Other interesting text-formatting properties of CSS include letter-spacing, which controls the space between letters, and text-shadow, which produces a basic drop shadow effect. You'll find information about all the CSS properties on the W3C CSS page at www.w3.org/Style/CSS, but be wary of the lesser-known properties – not all browsers understand them.

# Margins, padding and borders

The space around different elements of XHTML is controlled by CSS's margin and padding properties, while border properties allow you to draw a variety of different outlines around blocks of text and images.

**The difference between margin (top) and padding (below).**

## Margins and padding

The CSS margin and padding properties both control space around content. They work similarly and are easily confused, but there is a subtle difference between the two: while margins create space around the outside of an element, padding adds space to the inside of an element.

**Margins and padding in action**

The two illustrations on this page show the effect of applying margin and padding to the header division of our template. In the CSS file, the unique id of the header division is used as our selector. Note that the id must be prefixed by a hash symbol. To make the effect of the margins and padding more obvious, the header has also been given a background colour:

```
#header {
    background-color: #F93;
    margin: 50px;
}
```

In the top illustration, the margin setting results in a 50-pixel wide margin that separates the header division from everything around it. In the bottom illustration, 50 pixels of padding are applied instead:

```
#header {
    background-color: #F93;
    padding: 50px;
}
```

This time, the extra space is added to the internal boundaries, creating space around the top level heading inside the division while leaving the margins around the division itself unchanged.

**Setting variable margins and padding**

In the examples above, `margin` and `padding` properties set equal spacing around or inside all four sides of the element to which they are applied. To set a value for one side only, use the `margin-left`, `margin-right`, `margin-top`, and `margin-bottom` or `padding-left`, `padding-right`, `padding-top`, and `padding-bottom` properties instead. You can set any number of margin and padding properties. If you are setting multiple values, you can reduce the size of your code using the following shorthand versions of the `margin` property, which works in exactly the same way if you substitute `margin` for `padding`:

`margin: 6em;`

Sets a 6em margin around all sides of the element to which it is applied.

`margin: 3em 6em 9em 12em;`

Sets a 3em margin to the top, 6em to the right, 9em to the bottom and 12em to the left of the element to which it is applied.

`margin: 6em;`

`margin: 3em 6em 9em 12em;`

# 5 Using CSS

`margin`: 3em 6em;

`margin`: 3em 6em 9em;

There is now unwanted space at the top of the page.

`margin`: 3em 6em;

Sets a 3em margin to the top and bottom and a 6em margin to the left and right of the element to which it is applied.

`margin`: 3em 6em 9em;

Sets a 3em margin to the top, a 6em margin to the left and right and a 9em margin to the bottom of the element to which it is applied.

**Applying margins to the page itself**

By using the body tag of your XHTML file as a selector, margin and padding values can be set for the page itself in relation to the browser window. The rule below removes the page margins from our Camden Canteen site completely, so allowing the content to extend right up to the edge of the browser window:

```
body {
  margin: 0;
}
```

**Troubleshooting**

Despite removing all the space around the body element, there is still some unwanted space to the top of our logo image. To achieve the design shown in our mock-up, this space must be closed. The culprit is the h1 tag within which our logo is nested. In the absence of any other instruction, the browser is using its default settings to style the h1 tag. A new rule targeting only the h1 tag overrides this behaviour:

```
h1 {
  margin: 0;
}
```

**must know**

If you experience a problem, checking your code will almost certainly get to the root of it. Test your page frequently in as many browsers as possible too, and try validating your code to highlight potential problems. If fixing the issue requires a change to your XHTML or CSS file, then consider adding an explanatory comment (see pages 81 and 98) to help you understand your method when you come back to the code later.

**The gap has been closed and the page now matches the mock-up.**

## Using a container to centre content

By default, browsers will display in the left of the browser window. This can lead to large blank spaces on the right of the screen when fixed-width pages are viewed in larger browser windows. Splitting the extra space between both sides of the screen, with the main content sitting in the middle of the browser window, makes it all look much more elegant. It is easy to achieve this effect by using the margin property.

## Container technique

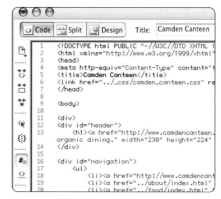

**1** First, we need to group all the main content within one new division. In the XHTML document, add an opening `<div>` tag immediately after the `<body>` tag and a closing `</div>` immediately before the closing `</body>` tag. All our content is now nested within this new division.

**2** To select the new division with CSS, it must have a unique identification. Add the `id` attribute to the opening `<div>` tag and use it to name the division. Divisions used for this technique are often called `container` or `wrapper`, but you can choose any name that isn't used elsewhere.

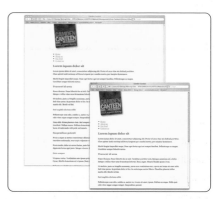

**3** Return to the CSS file and create a new rule to target the new division. Use the width property to set a `width` in either absolute or relative units, and then add the `margin` property with a value of `auto`. The width chosen for the Camden Canteen design is 750px.

**4** Save both the XHTML and CSS documents before opening the XHTML file in your browser. The main content now occupies the width assigned to the new division, and the equal blank space on either side automatically expands and contracts as you resize the browser window.

**5** To match the mock-up, change the page background colour (specified in the CSS rule applied to our body tag) from #FFC (cream) to #9C6 (green). Then specify a cream background colour for the new wrapper division.

**6** Finally, to separate the text from the edge of the wrapper division, add a left and right padding declaration of 20px to the CSS rules for the heading and paragraph elements.

# Borders

The border properties of CSS allow you to control the style, width, colour and location of any border you apply to XHTML elements.

## Basic borders

The `border-style` property with a value of `solid` provides a quick way to outline a particular element. More interesting border styles can be achieved using values such as `dotted`, `dashed` or `groove`. You can also use the `none` value to ensure browsers don't apply any borders of their own. Some browsers apply a border to all images nested within a hyperlink. This rule removes borders from all XHTML `img` elements:

```
img {
    border: none;
}
```

**did you know?**
This technique isn't strictly semantic, since the purpose of the container division is only presentational. However, it's a relatively mild indiscretion.

### Border width

Use the `border-width` property to specify the exact width of your border. The value can be given in either absolute or relative units, or it can simply be described as either thin, medium or thick. It is generally easier to set borders in absolute numbers of pixels.

**The CSS for this border is the same, yet the display differs depending on the browser used.**

### Border colour

The colour of a border can be set using the `border-color` property. As with background and text colours, the value of this property can be either one of the sixteen predefined colours listed earlier or an RGB or hexadecimal reference. Try to stick to web- safe colours where possible, especially for thin borders.

**The footer's top border separates it from the content above.**

## Border location

The border properties discussed so far affect all sides of the element to which they are applied, but in many cases you will only want to create a border on one side. Adding either -top, -bottom, -left or -right to the border declaration makes this possible. The rule below, for example, adds a 1 pixel solid black border below every second level heading on the page:

```
h2 {
    border-bottom-width: 1px;
    border-bottom-style: solid;
    border-bottom-color: #000;
}
```

## Border shorthand

As with margins and padding, you can simplify the code for a border by specifying a border's width, style and colour in one property. Thus the previous example could also be written as:

```
h2 {
    border-bottom: 1px solid #000;
}
```

**must know**

The same principle applies to the
border-left,
border-right,
border-top and
border properties.

# The box model

Margins, padding and borders give you a great deal of control over the more complicated layouts. The way in which they all come together around an individual element of XHTML is summarized by the so-called box model.

The box model can be complicated and its finer points are beyond the scope of this book. One aspect

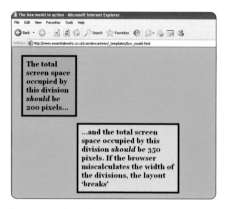

Internet Explorer 6

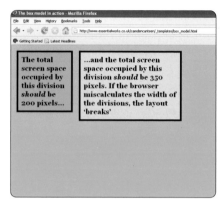

Firefox

Internet Explorer 6 and older versions misinterpret the box model, meaning that the two divisions in this example don't line up as intended, so 'breaking' the design.

we do need to understand, however, relates to how the overall width or height of any one XHTML element (or 'box') is calculated.

The illustration on this page represents a division called box. It has a set width, as well as margins, padding and borders. The CSS applied to it might look something like this:

```
#box {
    width: 150px;
    margin: 10px;
    padding: 10px;
    border: 5px solid #000;
}
```

**must know**
If the intricacies of the box model are causing problems, you can consult the official explanation of its inner workings at www.w3.org/TR/REC -CSS2/box.html

According to the box model, the overall width or height occupied by this division is the sum of all these elements. Its width, for example, would be 10 (left margin) + 5 (left border) + 10 (left padding) + 150 (division width) + 10 (right padding) + 5 (right margin) + 10 (right margin) = 200 pixels. Once you understand this, working out the required dimensions for the nested elements of more complicated layouts becomes much easier. If the cumulative widths of nested elements do not equal the width of the element with which they are contained, the layout may not fit together as you had expected.

## Internet Explorer and the box model

Unfortunately, all but the most recent version of Internet Explorer are prone to misunderstand the box model. Instead of adding the width of margins, padding and borders to the stated width of an element, Internet Explorer would include the padding and borders within the element's own width. Thus the box division in the previous example would occupy only 170 pixels.

This behaviour can wreak havoc on even the most carefully planned designs, and web developers have come up with all sorts of tricks or 'hacks' to get round the problem. Most of these exploit additional idiosyncracies in Internet Explorer's behaviour in order to give it different CSS to that seen by less troublesome browsers, so that the display of a website ultimately appears the same on all browsers. Hacks, however, are complicated and their shelf life may be curtailed when new versions of browsers fix the bugs upon which they depend. A much easier option is to always use a strict document type. This way, at least the two most recent versions of Internet Explorer will always comply with the box model in the correct way.

**must know**

Using a strict doctype will not force earlier versions of Internet Explorer to change their errant ways. If your site's audience is likely to be using these older versions, try to avoid setting padding and margins on elements for which you are also declaring a width value. For example, instead of applying width and padding to a division, apply only the width to the division and apply padding to the paragraphs nested inside the division instead.

# The CSS display property

CSS's display property offers three different ways of displaying each element of a page's XHTML code. In most cases, you can rely on each element's default behaviour to display content as you intend it. Sometimes, however, you will need to override the default by explcitly stating an alternative value for display.

## Values for the display property

The two most important display values are:

**Block** The vast majority of XHTML tags display as block-level elements by default. This means that each element is considered to be a distinct block of content, each displayed below the preceding element. Headings and paragraphs written in XHTML are good examples of block-level elements.

**Inline** By contrast, inline-level elements are considered to be components of a distinct block of content, so they don't display as a separate block. The <em> and </em> tags used to italicize text within a paragraph are an example of an XHTML element that displays as an inline-level element by default.

In this screen grab, the Firefox web developer toolbar has been used to outline all the block-level elements on the page.

## The display property in action

On the Camden Canteen mock-up, our navigation links are displayed in a horizontal row across the top of the page. On our live page, however, each link appears as a bulleted list item. To match the live page to the mock-up, therefore, we need to change the display setting of each list item from block (its default) to inline.

# Creating an inline list

1

2

```
#navigation li {
    display: inline;
}
```

Open the CSS style sheet and add the code as it is shown above. This creates a new rule targetting all list items within our navigation division and setting the display property to `inline`. Viewed in a browser, our list items now appear in a horizontal row.

```
#navigation {
    background-color: #063;
    font: bold 1.0em/1.5em Arial,
Helvetica, sans-serif;
    text-transform: uppercase;
    text-align: right;
    padding: 0 30px;
}
```

To match the mock-up, we also need to restyle the unordered list element. The rule above sets values for the entire list's background colour, font, weight, case, text colour, case, alignment and padding.

## did you know?

Another value for the display property is `none`, which effectively hides the XHTML to which it is applied. Use it sparingly – search engines may refuse to index sites with hidden content, since it can be used as a crude attempt to improve a site's ranking. For more on search engines, see Chapter 7.

## must know

Using just `li` and `ul` as the selectors here would target all the list items and unordered lists on the page. That's not desirable here, since we still want unordered lists within the main body to retain their default formatting as bulleted, block-level lists.

3

```
#navigation a {
    color: #FFF;
    text-decoration: none;
}
```

To make the navigation links white, we need to override the green link colours set for the rest of the page and remove the underline. The rule above targets only links (XHTML anchor elements) within the navigation division.

4

Finally, go back to the list item rule and set a value for the **margin-left** property. This creates some space between each item, which makes the different navigation options distinct and matches the original mock-up.

### Variations on a theme

You can now use a similar technique to make the links in the footer, creating an inline list that matches the design on the mock-up.

```
#footer li {
    display: inline;
    margin-right: 1em;
}
```

In this way, using CSS to style a list of navigation links combines exemplary accessibility with endless creative potential. (See www.alvit.de/css-showcase for examples of what the display property can do.)

# Floats

The rather oddly named CSS float property is used to control the alignment of XHTML elements in relation to their surrounding elements. It's a surprisingly powerful little piece of code.

## Basic floats

The two core values for the float property are simple: left and right. An obvious use for them is to position images within text. Designers often create rules like the one below to align XHTML elements:

```
.left {
    float: left;
}
```

**The images on this page are floated to the left of their accompanying text.**

This rule can then be applied to multiple XHTML elements using the class attribute. The XHTML code below, for example, applies the rule to an image nested within a paragraph:

```
<p><img src="../_images/graphic.gif"
class="left" />Lorem ipsum dolor sit amet,
consectetuer adipiscing elit.</p>
```

## Clear

The float property works hand-in-hand with the clear property. If the float property controls how neighbouring elements should flow around the element to which it is applied, clear *prevents* other elements floating to one or both sides of the targetted element.

**must know**

These rules are called classes. Instead of using an XHTML element as a selector, classes use the class attribute of one or more XHTML elements to apply CSS rules to them. In the CSS file, classes are designated by the full stop before their name.

# Creating layouts with floats

Floats are useful tools for positioning images, but it is when they are used as a layout technique that floats really come into their own.

## Using floats to create two columns

**1** Open your XHTML document and make sure that each of the content divisions has a unique ID attribute. To create the layout shown on the original mock-up, we will apply new CSS rules to the main, related and footer divisions.

**2** Now switch to your CSS document and add two new rules targetting the main and related divisions. Use the **width** property to set the width of each one. According to the original mock-up, the related division (which will become the left-hand column) is 250px wide and the main division 500px wide.

**3** To position the columns, we need to declare a value for the float property of each division. Set the main division to float to the **right**, and the related division to float to the **left**.

**4** Check the result in a browser. Though the columns have been created, things are clearly not quite as they should be yet!

```
73      float: left;
74      width: 250px;
75  }
76
77  #footer {
78      border-top: 1px solid #666;
79      clear: both;
80  }
81
82  /* Navigation division CSS */
83
84  #navigation li {
85      display: inline;
86      margin-left: 1em;
87  }
88
89  #navigation a {
90      color: #FFF;
91      text-decoration: none;
92  }
93
```

**5** Clearing the footer out of the way will fix the problem. In the CSS file, add a new declaration to the rule that targets the footer division, setting the `clear` property to `both`.

**6** Now the page displays as intended.

This is just one example of the myriad layouts that can be achieved using CSS techniques. The beauty of CSS is that once the basic XHTML page has been created, the layout of its content can be changed with only a few edits to the CSS document. This is why the names originally used to identify the different divisions in the XHTML document were chosen based on their content, not their appearance in the mock-up. A division called `left_column` wouldn't make much sense if you subsquently decided to position that element on the right.

**These sites depend on the float property for their layouts.**

# Precision positioning

One of the most celebrated features of CSS is its ability to position elements with pixel-perfect precision.

If your design depends on the exact placement of particular items, CSS's position property – and the top, left, bottom and right properties that work with it – could be the answer to your prayers. Use the position property to determine where an element's position should be measured from, and then set the distance an element appears from that point by declaring a value for one or more of the top, left, bottom and right properties.

**Positioning in practise**

Example 1

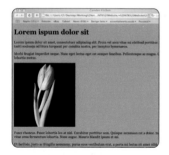

**Example 1**

```
#flower {
    position: static;
}
```

This rule declares that the position of the image be static. This is the default state, so the rule has no real effect – the image displays exactly where it appears in the XHTML (in this case, between two paragraphs).

Example 2

```
#flower {
    position: relative;
    left: 300px;
}
```

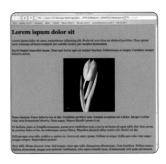

**Example 2**

Relative positioning places an element in relation
to where it would have been had no position
declarations been made. In this case, 300 pixels are
added to the image's left-hand co-ordinates,
causing it to move to the right by that amount.

Example 3

```
#flower {
    position: absolute;
    left: 300px;
}
```

**Example 3**

Absolute positioning with the same value for the
left property has a similar effect, except that the
image co-ordinates are now measured in relation to
the XHTML element within which the image is
contained – in this case the page body. As a result,
the text no longer flows around the image but is
obscured beneath it.

Example 4

```
#flower {
    position: fixed;
    top: 100px;
    left: 100px;
}
```

**Example 4**

Fixed positions are measured from the top left corner of the browser window. The rule above positions the flower image 100 pixels from the top left-hand corner. Note that the position of fixed elements is entirely independent of all other items on the page, so the image doesn't move if the user scrolls down to the bottom of the page.

### Negative position values

You can change the direction in which the item moves as a result of positioning declarations by setting negative values. We can use this feature to move the navigation division of the Camden Canteen site towards the top of the browser window, so that its position matches that shown on the mock-up. First, its position is declared to be relative. Then, the top property is given a value of -100px.

**Using negative position values to move the navigation division.**

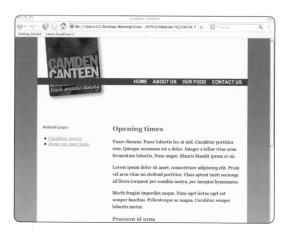

### Setting the z-index

Unfortunately, moving the navigation division creates a new problem. Though it has moved up the

Setting the z-index.

screen, the navigation menu now obscures the logo. To bring the top level heading (within which the logo is enclosed) to the front, we must expand the rule targetting the h1 element:

```
h1 {
    margin: 0;
    position: relative;
    z-index: 1;
}
```

In addition to specifying relative positioning for this element, the rule now also sets the heading's z-index. The z-index property provides a way of specifying an element's position in a pile of overlapping elements. The value you state depends on the value set for any other overlapping elements. In this case, no z-index value is declared for the navigation division, so a value of 1 – effectively one higher than the z-index of the navigation division – is enough to bring the logo back to the fore.

## want to know more?

• Find out how to create different style sheets for different media at www.howtocreate. co.uk/tutorials/css/ mediatypes
• You'll find some beautifully presented advanced advice on web typography at www.webtypography. net
• For more ideas on being creative with lists and CSS, see the excellent examples at www.css.maxdesign. com.au
• If the complexities of coding are getting you down, visit a CSS showcase like www.cssremix.com or www.bestwebgallery. com to remind yourself of the potential fruits of your labours.

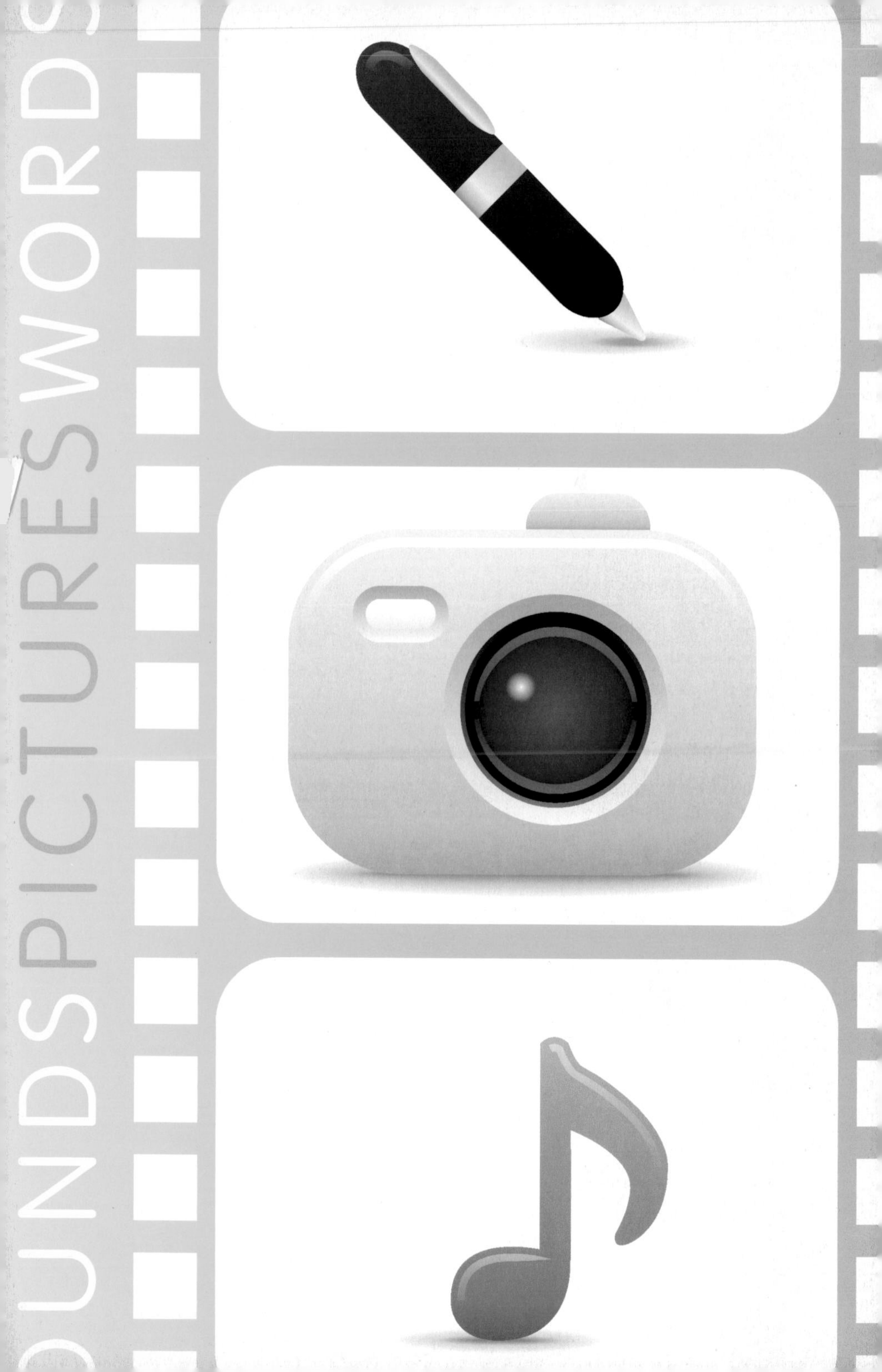
PICTURESWORDS

# 6 Graphics on the web

Striking pictures and illustrations are a great way to make your site stand out from the crowd. In this chapter, you will learn more about the different graphics formats used on the web and discover how to optimize images for display online. And for a truly slick finish, you will pick up a couple of quick and easy ways to make your homepage handiwork look like the work of a seasoned professional.

# Graphics formats

The three main graphics formats used on the web are GIF, JPEG and PNG. Any image used on your site will need to be saved in one of these formats, so make sure you understand their different characteristics.

**By saving this illustration as a transparent GIF, the pink background colour specified by the web page's CSS shows through. In the non-transparent version, the empty parts of the image appear as white.**

### GIF files

Graphics Interchange Format (GIF) files were originally developed by the internet service provider CompuServe. They have since become a standard format for web graphics, thanks to their small file size. Key to the GIF's success is its ability to reduce an image to a limited number of colours. GIFs are most often used to save logos and other simple illustrations, 'snapping' all the colours of the original image to their nearest web-safe equivalents.

GIFs are often used to create images with transparent backgrounds, where the page's background colour shows through the 'empty' areas of the graphic. They can also be used to create basic animations.

### JPEG files

JPEG files are named after the Joint Photographic Experts Group that first created them. As the name suggests, they are most suited to the large number of colours and subtle textures typical of photographic images. Like GIF files, JPEGs use compression technology to achieve small file sizes. Unlike GIF files, JPEGs do not support transparency and do not allow for the colour palette to be restrained to web-safe colours.

## PNG files

The PNG or Portable Network Graphic is the (relatively) new kid on the block. Born of a legal dispute surrounding CompuServe's GIF format, the capabilities of the PNG outshine those of its older cousin. It's particularly useful for creating smooth transparency effects. Unlike GIF files, PNG images can contain areas of partial transparency, opening up a whole range of creative possibilities.

Unfortunately, web browsers have been slow to catch on to the full potential of the PNG. Though the format works well in most modern browsers, PNG transparency does not work in all but the most recent version of Internet Explorer for the PC.

**The PNG format's capacity for semi-transparent pixels makes it ideal for the smooth drop shadow in the Camden Canteen logo. The effect remains smooth even when the background colour is changed.**

# Preparing graphics

Optimizing your graphics for the web allows you to control the way colours are displayed, and ensures that the images on your sites do not bring its loading time to a snail's pace.

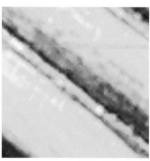

**Only 72 pixels per inch are required to create a smooth image on screen.**

## Factors to consider

Making graphics web-friendly is a balancing act between image quality and download time. The key variables are:

**Image size and resolution**

Place a GIF, JPEG or PNG file under a microscope and you will see that it is made up of a pattern of coloured squares, or pixels. The number of pixels in a given physical space is the image's resolution, usually measured in pixels per inch (ppi). In printed documents, a very high number of pixels per inch is required to create the illusion of smooth curves. On screen, much lower resolutions are sufficient. To minimize download times, change image resolution to 72ppi and reduce the physical size of the file to match the space that it should occupy on screen.

**Colour palette**

Reducing the number of colours in a GIF image will always decrease file size, but proceed with caution: limit the colour palette too drastically and your image will appear blocky and lacking in detail. Images with limited colour palettes are said to be 'indexed', so look for this setting in your graphics application.

# The easy way to save for web

Many graphics applications have special features dedicated to optimizing images for web use. Here, Photoshop's 'Save for Web & Devices' feature is used to save a GIF and a JPEG.

## Saving a graphic

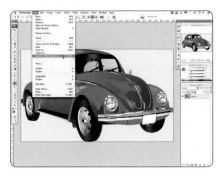

**1** Open the original image, or create it from scratch. When you are ready to save a copy for web use, choose 'Save for Web & Devices' (or in older versions 'Save for Web') from the file menu.

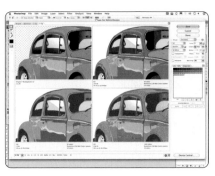

**2** The dialogue box lets you compare the results of different settings side-by-side against the original. Choose a display option by clicking one of the tabs in the top left. The active image – the one to which the settings shown on the right are applied – is outlined. Click on a different version to tweak its settings.

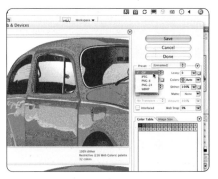

**3** With one of the optimized versions active, choose the file type you would like the image to be saved as from the drop-down menu on the right. This image contains areas of flat colour, best suited to the GIF format.

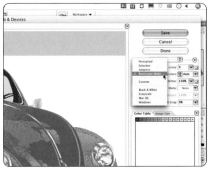

**4** Experiment with the settings. The most important drop-down, located just below the file format, switches between various ways of reducing the number of colours in the image. 'Restrictive (Web)' limits the palette to web-safe colours only.

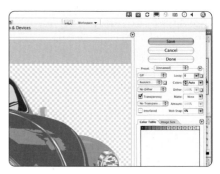

**5** Try the different dithering options from the drop-down menu located underneath the file type menu. Deliberate dithering can simulate colours that are being removed from the image, helping to retain detail.

**6** To make the image transparent, tick the transparency box. Don't worry too much about the transparency dither setting – you can usually leave it set to 'No Transparency Dither'.

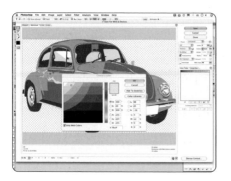

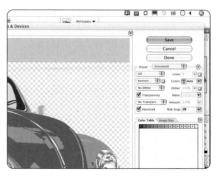

**7** Though pixels can't be semi-transparent in a GIF file, you can create a slightly more seamless transparency by choosing a 'Matte' colour to match the background of the page on which the graphic will appear. The edge of your image is blended into the matte colour, creating the illusion of a smoother transition from foreground to background.

**8** Tick the 'Interlaced' box to change the way your image loads. Non-interlaced images appear in the browser in-lines of pixels, starting from the top of the image, until the complete graphic has loaded. Interlaced images load pixels from across the whole image, adding more and more detail until the complete image has loaded. Note that interlacing increases file size.

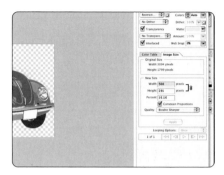

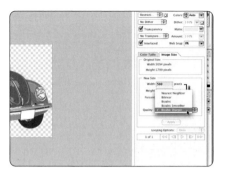

**9** Next, click on the 'Image Size' tab to reduce the dimensions of your graphic to the required size. Make sure the 'Constrain Proportions' box is ticked before entering either the width or height of the space the graphic is to fill (measured in pixels). Photoshop automatically adjusts the other value so that the image is not squashed or stretched out of shape.

**10** The 'Quality' drop-down determines how Photoshop removes pixels in order to reduce the image's dimensions. In most cases, 'Bicubic Sharper' is the one to choose. If your image has hard edges between different colours, try 'Nearest Neighbor'. There's no resolution setting to worry about – Photoshop will automatically save a 72ppi file.

**11** When you are happy with the preview image, click save to save it in your site's images folder. Before saving the final image, make sure the version you want is the active (outlined) image. Otherwise, you will save one of the other versions by mistake.

### must know

If you are creating a graphic that includes text, look for the 'anti-aliasing' setting in your graphics application. This blurs the edges of type slightly, preventing it from appearing jagged on screen.

### Saving a PNG

You can also save PNG files using 'Save for Web & Devices'. There are in fact two types of PNG files. The options for PNG-8 files are like those for GIFs. The PNG-24 format, meanwhile, is useful for its even more sophisticated transparency options, but beware of its larger file sizes.

### Saving a JPEG

Photographs are best saved as JPEG files. Luckily, the options in 'Save for Web & Devices' are simpler than those for GIF files.

## Saving a photograph

**1** Open your original image and make any adjustments. When you're ready, bring up the 'Save for Web & Devices' box from the File menu.

**2** Select JPEG as the file type and experiment with the preset quality settings. You can fine-tune the result by adjusting the numerical quality slider to the right. Lower settings will result in faster downloads, so go as low as you dare without overly compromising image quality.

**3** The 'Progressive' box is similar to the 'Interlaced' option for GIF files. Unlike GIF interlacing, however, this option does not increase file size. Tick the box with confidence!

**4** You can use the 'Blur' slider to counter the effects of reducing image quality. Slightly blurring an optimized JPEG hides the 'blocky' appearance that is sometimes introduced by the compression applied to it.

**5** Don't worry about the other colour settings. Instead, switch to the image size tab and set the optimized photograph's size in the same way as for GIF images.

**6** Save the final JPEG in your site's images folder.

---

**did you know?**

Adobe's 'Save for Web' feature is available in several Adobe applications, including the budget Photoshop Elements program.

Users of the free GIMP application can download a similar 'Save for Web' plug-in from http://registry. gimp.org/plugin?id=8799

# Using stock images

Knowing how to put graphics online is one thing, but producing great photographs and illustrations in the first place is quite another. If your creative skills are lagging behind your technical prowess, a new breed of stock image libraries is ready to help.

## Introducing microstock

Agencies that license the work of professional photographers and illustrators to publishers are nothing new. But the cost of stock images has traditionally been beyond the reach of smaller businesses or private individuals. Now, however, a group of new agencies – known as 'microstock' libraries – have opened their doors to amateur and semi-professional contributors and made vast numbers of images available for as little as $1.

### How it works

Microstock agencies like iStockphoto (www.istock photo.com), Dreamstime (www.dreamstime.com) and Shutterstock (www.shutterstock.com) are

iStockphoto is the original microstock agency. There are now over 2 million photographs and illustrations in its library, and more are added daily.

entirely web-based. The sites' powerful search functions make it easy to find all manner of images, and the best sites vet every image contributed to make sure that poorly exposed, out-of-focus photographs and crudely drawn illustrations don't make it into the 'agency'. Typically, purchasers buy either a monthly subscription or an inexpensive block of credits that can be redeemed against images within a set time period.

## Free images

For those on a real budget, sites like stock.xchang (www.sxc.hu) and Stockvault (www.stockvault.net) go one step further with their libraries of entirely free pictures. It may be a little harder to find what you are looking for, but it's always worth a try.

## A word of caution

Used carefully, stock imagery can dramatically enhance the visual appeal of your site and lift it above its competitors. Used indiscriminately, it can bury your core content in an ill-conceived melange of visual distraction. Bear these tips in mind:

• Get a clear idea of the image you are looking for before you start searching for it, and resist the temptation to download graphics that don't really fit your site's design or content.

• Try to maintain a consistent illustrative or photographic style throughout your site. Aim for a body of images that appear to belong together.

• Avoid visual clichés. Your office may be equipped with a telephone, but do you really need that posed picture of a smiling, headset-bearing telephonist? Probably not.

**watch out!**

When you download a stock image, you will need to agree to a licence for its use. Certain uses may be restricted, or you might have to inform the copyright holder about how you have used their work. Don't break the terms of the licence and never infringe another person's copyright.

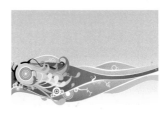

**Microstock images are great for icons, backgrounds, features and conceptual illustrations.**

# Decorative backgrounds

You already know how to include images in a site's content, but with CSS you can also use them as decorative backgrounds for XHTML elements. This popular technique is not difficult to use.

## Adding a background image

On the Camden Canteen site, the CSS background-color property was applied to the body element of the XHTML document to create the green page background visible behind the container division (which was, in turn, given its own cream-coloured background). But in the original mock-up, the page background is a gentle gradient from dark to light green. To achieve this effect on the live site, we will create a graphic of the gradient effect and use CSS to display it as the page background.

### Creating the gradient graphic

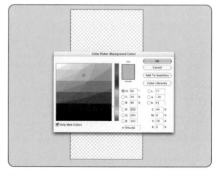

**1** Open a new blank document in your graphics application. Choose a resolution of 72ppi and, if there is a 'Color Mode' option, select RGB. For the height, enter a number in pixels equal to the point at which you wish your gradient to end. Here, the gradient will end 1000 pixels down the page.

**2** Use the colour picker to select two colours for the gradient. The colour at the lower end of the gradient should be the same as the solid colour specified for your page background.

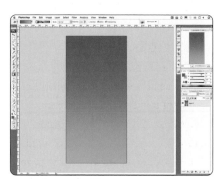

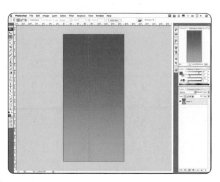

**3** Switch to the Gradient tool and set it to use the two colours chosen. Then, draw a gradient from the top to the bottom of your document. Make sure that the gradient ends within the document's boundaries – otherwise the transition to the lower colour will not be complete.

**4** Before you save the final graphic, use the crop tool to cut it down to an image that is just 1 pixel wide (leaving the height unchanged). Rather than display the uncropped image, CSS will be used to repeat or 'tile' the cropped version as many times as is necessary to fill the browser window. This keeps download times to a minimum.

**5** Now save an optimized copy of the gradient image in your site's images folder. Use the PNG-24 format (without transparency) to maintain the smoothness of the gradient with reliable colours.

**must know**

If you used a graphics application to create your original mock-up, you can jump straight to step 4 by cropping your existing mock-up to a 1-pixel wide section of gradient, and saving an optimized copy of the resulting image. Be careful not to overwrite your original mock-up, though!

## Writing the CSS rules

**1** With the gradient ready to use, go back to your CSS style sheet and locate the rule for the body element. Check that the solid colour already declared with the `background-color` property matches the colour at the bottom of your gradient image. This colour will be visible where the length of the page begins to excede the height of the gradient image. Matching it to the bottom of the gradient image creates a seamless transition.

```
⬤ ⬤ ⬤                                        camden_canteen
  1   @charset "UTF-8";
  2   /* CSS Document for Camden Canteen website, sample proje
      Your Own Website" */
  3
  4   /* Blanket styles */
  5
  6   body {
  7       color: #000;
  8       background-color:#9C6;
  9       font-family: Georgia, Times-New-Roman, serif;
 10       margin: 0;
 11       padding: 0;
 12   }
 13
 14   img {
 15       border: none;
 16   }
 17
 18   h1, h2, h3, h4, h5, h6 {
 19       color: #363;
 20       padding: 0 20px;
 21   }
 22
 23   h1 {
 24       margin: 0;
 25       position: relative;
 26       z-index: 1;
 27   }
 28
 29   p {
 30       font-size: 1em;
 31       line-height: 1.5em;
 32       padding: 0 20px;
 33   }
```

**2** Add a new declaration to the body rule using the `background-image` property. The value of this property should state the location of the gradient image. In this case, the value is `url(../_images/background.png)`

```
⬤ ⬤ ⬤                                        camden_canteen
  1   @charset "UTF-8";
  2   /* CSS Document for Camden Canteen website, sample proje
      Your Own Website" */
  3
  4   /* Blanket styles */
  5
  6   body {
  7       color: #000;
  8       background-color:#9C6;
  9       background-image:url(../_images/background.png);
 10       font-family: Georgia, Times-New-Roman, serif;
 11       margin: 0;
 12       padding: 0;
 13   }
 14
 15   img {
 16       border: none;
 17   }
 18
 19   h1, h2, h3, h4, h5, h6 {
 20       color: #363;
 21       padding: 0 20px;
 22   }
 23
 24   h1 {
 25       margin: 0;
 26       position: relative;
 27       z-index: 1;
 28   }
 29
 30   p {
 31       font-size: 1em;
 32       line-height: 1.5em;
 33       padding: 0 20px;
```

**3** Save the CSS file and open an associated XHTML file in your browser. By default, the browser fills the entire background by repeating the background image both horizontally and vertically – fine for background images that repeat in both directions, but not the effect required here.

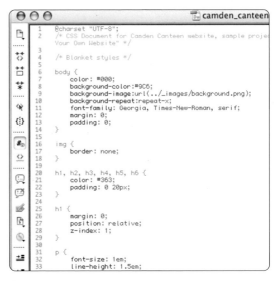

```
          camden_canteen
1    @charset "UTF-8";
2    /* CSS Document for Camden Canteen website, sample proje
     Your Own Website" */
3
4    /* Blanket styles */
5
6    body {
7        color: #000;
8        background-color:#9C6;
9        background-image:url(../_images/background.png);
10       background-repeat:repeat-x;
11       font-family: Georgia, Times-New-Roman, serif;
12       margin: 0;
13       padding: 0;
14   }
15
16   img {
17       border: none;
18   }
19
20   h1, h2, h3, h4, h5, h6 {
21       color: #363;
22       padding: 0 20px;
23   }
24
25   h1 {
26       margin: 0;
27       position: relative;
28       z-index: 1;
29   }
30
31   p {
32       font-size: 1em;
33       line-height: 1.5em;
```

**4** Go back to the CSS rule for the body element and add a new property called **background-repeat**. The possible values are **background-repeat** (which displays the image once in the top left of the browser window), repeat-x (to repeat horizontally) and repeat-y (to repeat vertically). In this case, choose repeat-x.

**5** Check the result in the browser. The effect is now complete.

Decorative backgrounds | 155

## More background tricks

For more sophisticated background effects, try these additional background properties.

### Background attachment

Use the background-attachment property on the body element to determine how the background image behaves when the page is scrolled. With a value of scroll, the background moves with the rest of the page. Set to fixed, and the background maintains its original position, with the rest of the content scrolling over it.

### Background position

The background-position property allows more precise control over the position of the background image in relation to the element to which it is applied. Its value can take one of three formats:

**In words** as a vertical alignment (top, center or bottom) followed by a horizontal position (left, center or right). Thus a value of top right positions a background image in the top right-hand corner of the element to which it is applied. If the position is only stated for one plain, browsers automatically place the background in the centre of the other plain.

**In pixels** based on the co-ordinates of the top left-hand corner of the target XHTML element being 0 0, a value of x5 y10 would place the background image 5 pixels along that element's x-axis and 10 pixels down its y-axis. If a position is only specified in one direction, browsers position the background image half way along the other axis.

**must know**

Remember that background properties are not limited to the body element. You can also apply them to other tags, such as divisions, table cells, list items and links (in all their various states). On the Camden Canteen site the 3D effect behind the main navigation is created by a tiling background image applied to the navigation division.

**As a percentage** if the target elements x and y axes begin at 0 per cent and end at 100 per cent, a value of x25% y50% would place the background image a quarter of the way along that element's x-axis and half way down its y-axis. Again, if a position is only declared for one axis, the value of for the other is assumed to be 50 per cent.

## Background shorthand

The background property means you can set values for all the background properties at once. The values for the shorthand background property are those that would otherwise have been given separately for background-color, background-image, background-repeat, background-attachment, and background-position. There's no need to specify all these values, but those that are specified must be listed in this order. Thus the shorthand version of the background declaration for the body element of the Camden Canteen site would be:

```
body {
    background: #9C6
url(../_images/background.png) repeat-x
fixed;
}
```

**These striking and visually varied sites make good use of the CSS background properties.**

# Basic GIF animations

While jaw-dropping Flash interfaces are likely to prove too demanding for the novice developer, the ability of the GIF file format to create simple animations is much easier to exploit.

## How GIF animation works

An animated GIF contains not just one image, but a series of graphics which are displayed one after the other. Each individual graphic is called a 'frame', and the animation works in just the same way as an old-fashioned cartoon or flick-through animation. By making a minor change to each frame and then playing all the frames in sequence, a moving image is created.

It is much easier to animate a computer-generated illustration when each of its elements is isolated on a separate layer.

**Creating an animated GIF**

**1** In this Photoshop document, each element of the illustration sits on its own layer. Moving the layers, or turning them on and off, is a simple way to set up the different frames of our animation.

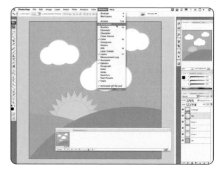

**2** First, bring up the animation palette. In Photoshop, this shows all the frames in the animation and allows frames to be added or deleted. The first frame is created automatically.

**3** Add a new frame by clicking on the white blank document icon. This duplicates the previous frame. To make the new frame different from the previous, click on it in the animations palette to select, then adjust the main Photoshop document.

**4** Keep adding new frames until the animation is complete. Using a large number of frames with only minor alterations to each one will create a smoother animation, although the final file size will be bigger.

**5** Press the play button on the animation palette to preview the animation. You can adjust the length of time each frame is displayed using the drop-down menu underneath each one in the animation palette.

**6** The drop-down menu in the bottom left corner of the animation palette allows you to specify whether the animation should stop after it has first played, or continuously repeat. If you create a repeating animation, try to make the transition between the last frame and the first frame as seamless as that between any of the other frames.

**7** When you are happy with your animation, choose 'Save for Web & Devices' from the File menu to save it in GIF format. You can now link the graphic to your XHTML page, just as you did on page 88, and it will animate when displayed in the browser.

# Favicons

A favicon is a tiny graphical icon which browsers use to denote a website in their bookmark lists or in the address bar. Giving your site a Favicon all of its own is an easy way to keep up with the web's trendiest addresses.

**must know**
If correcting the relative file path of your favicon for every page of your site gets confusing, you can always enter the graphic's complete address. See pages 84–5 for a reminder of absolute and relative paths.

## Favicon fun and function

Open the 'Bookmarks' or 'Favourites' menu of your own web browser, and you will almost certainly find an array of colourful favicons (short for 'favourites icon') next to the names of sites you have bookmarked. When these customized graphics first started to appear among the list of bookmarked sites, the pages that wore them really stood out. Today, that novelty has largely worn off and the custom favicons can be little more visible than the

Different browsers use Favicons in different ways, but you can usually find them in the bookmarks list and in the browser's title bar.

default graphic that appears next to sites without their own symbol. Yet favicons are still a fun way to give an extra boost to your site's appearance.

## How to add a favicon

Essentially, favicons are a web graphic like any other. Use your graphics application to create your design, making sure it is square in format. The final favicon should be just 16 pixels wide and 16 pixels high, so simple designs generally work best. Save a copy of your final graphic as a GIF or PNG file (not JPEG). It's best to limit the colour palette to 216 colours. Older browsers prefer another file format, ICO, for favicons. Sites such as www.htmlkit.com/services/favicons will convert other graphics to ICO format for you.

### Linking the favicon

Once you have created the favicon, you then need to tell the browser where to find it. This is done by adding a few extra lines of code within the head element of every XHTML page to which the favicon belongs. There are various methods, but the W3C recommends adding the profile attribute to your opening head tag followed by a link element:

```
<head profile="http://www.w3.org/2005/11/
profile">
<link rel="icon" type="image/png"
href="../_images/favicon.png" />
```

You can get by without understanding this code in detail, but note that you will need to change the values of the type and href attributes to match the file type and location of your favicon.

**want to know more?**
- For more help with background colours, see Stripemania.com. This is a really useful site that allows you to create tiled backgrounds without the need for your own graphics software. A simple diagonal stripe can make a very effective background. On white, it can also be a good way to tone down the harshest web-safe colours, but make sure your text is still legible.
- Be careful with animation effects – in some circumstances they have been linked with photosensitive epilepsy. See the W3C's draft guidelines on this issue at: www.w3.org /TR/2005/WD-WCAG 20-20051123/guidelines. html#seizure

**Search ▶▶**

TRAFFIC

WARNINGS

INFO

RESOLUTIONS

LINKS

# 7 Getting the best out of your site

The web is a constantly evolving medium, and uploading your site to its server should not mark the end of its development. This chapter explores ways to improve your new site's performance and monitor its effectiveness. You will also learn about a simple way to sell advertising space and find out how to enhance your site's accessibility.

# Site analysis

The ability to step back and subject your site to measured criticism will be key to its long-term success. Anecdotal evidence combined with more scientific analysis paints a clear picture of your site's performance and can help you identify where it may be failing to meet its objectives.

## User testing

By far the best-qualified people to road test your new site are its target users. The specific needs of your audience should have been guiding the entire design process, so now is the time to find out how well you have been able to step into their shoes. Trawl your address book for suitable guinea pigs and watch them test your site to virtual destruction. Things to look out for include:

● How easily can users find what they are looking for? Are users trying to achieve tasks you had not expected your site to accomplish?

● If users cannot get what they want from your website, how close do they come? Fixing a broken link may be all you need to do.

● Which parts of the site draw the most attention? Are they also the bits you consider to be the most important?

● Is poor accessibility letting your site down? Illegible text and unsympathetic colours are typical complaints, or perhaps your site does not display correctly in the user's chosen browser?

**must know**

Flattery is great, but there's no point getting feedback from users who will only tell you what you want to hear. Your website must stand or fall on its own merits. Ask casual users of your site to send their comments too – you could set up an email link on your homepage.

# Site statistics

If your web host provides them, your site's statistics will provide cold, empirical data about the people who have actually visited your site. The statistics not only tell you how many visitors the site has had, but can also shed light on where they came from, which specific pages they viewed, how long they stayed and which browsers and operating systems they were using. Statistical information can also be gathered by a number of online services, notably Google Analytics.

## About Google Analytics

Google's free Analytics service stands out as much for the information it gathers about your site's users as it does for the intuitive and infinitely flexible ways in which it presents this data.

**must know**

You can use services like Google Analytics regardless of whether or not your site's host provides their own analytics package. Even if they do, you may find that other services are more comprehensive or easier to understand.

## Setting up a Google Analytics account

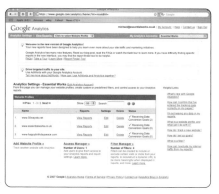

**1** Go to the Google Analytics site (www.google. com/analytics). If you already have a Google account, you can use it to log in to the Analytics service. Otherwise, follow the on-screen instructions to create one.

**2** You can use your account to analyze multiple websites. Each one has its own 'Profile'. To create a profile for your first site, click 'Add Website Profile' on the Analytics homepage.

**3** On the next page, enter your website address. For the Camden Canteen site, the address is http://www.camdencanteen.com. Select your local time zone and then click the 'Continue' button.

**4** Google Analytics now creates a special piece of code which you must add to every page of your site. Use your mouse to select the code and select 'Copy' from your browser's 'Edit' menu.

**5** Open one of your site's XHTML pages and locate the closing body tag, **</body>**. Place your cursor immediately before this tag, and choose 'Paste' from your editor's 'Edit' menu. This copies the Google tracking code to your page. Repeat the process for every page of your site before uploading them to your web server, replacing the existing versions.

**6** When you next log in to the Analytics site, check the status column next to your website profile. It takes around 24 hours for the status to change from 'Tracking code not detected' to 'Receiving Data'. If no data is being received after this time, check that you have added the code correctly.

## Filters

You can refine the data collected by Google Analytics using filters, which exclude certain visits from the statistics. For example, you could disregard visitors from a particular country or ignore visitors to particular sections of your site.

One particular function of filters is to exclude your *own* visits to your site, thus ensuring that the data displayed by Google Analytics is a true reflection of 'real' visitors.

If you connect to the internet using a fixed IP (Internet Protocol) address, you can use the step-by-step technique on the following page to filter out visits from that address. To find out whether or not your internet connection uses a fixed IP address, repeat the first step of the technique on different occasions. If the IP address shown changes, this means that it cannot be used as the basis for this filter. Consult the Google help pages for alternative methods. These are a little more complicated than the method shown here, but don't worry if they seem beyond you: unless your site is attracting hardly any visitors, the distortion caused by including your own visits will be relatively minimal.

## Using the Filter Manager

**1** First, you need to find out your IP address. Using the computer you wish to exclude from the Analytics data, visit a site like whatsmyip.org and note down the IP address shown.

**2** Now log in to Google Analytics again and click the Filter Manager link. This page shows all filters you have set up. To create a new filter, click 'Add Filter'.

**3** On the next page, choose a name for your filter and select 'Exclude all traffic from an IP address' from the 'Filter Type' drop-down menu. Then enter the IP address you noted earlier.

**4** The section below shows all the profiles you have created for your analytics account. Use the 'Add' button to choose the profiles to which the new filter should be applied. When done, click 'Finish'.

### Viewing and understanding Analytics data

The tracking code added to your site sends data back to Google on a daily basis. To view it, log in to Google Analytics and select your site's profile from the drop-down menu at the top of the page. Key

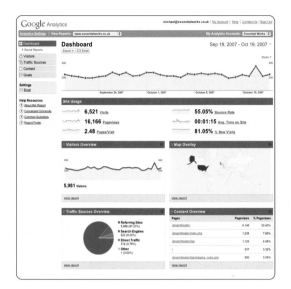

The Google Analytics Dashboard provides a convenient graphical overview of the data collected about visits to your site.

data is summarized on the 'Dashboard' page that now opens. Some particularly useful sections are:

**Site usage** This shows the total number of people who have visited your site, and gives you an overview of how far into your site they have delved. Visitor numbers are also shown over time in the chart at the top of the screen. Look out for the bounce rate, which shows the proportion of visitors who have left your site without viewing more than one page, and the percentage of new visitors. A high rate of return visitors indicates that your site has a loyal following!

**Map overlay** This section plots your visitors' physical location on a world map. It's particularly useful for businesses planning local advertising campaigns, and it can also reveal if a commercial site is attracting custom from areas it is unable to service. Click on the map to zoom in on individual countries.

**must know**

Understanding the
keywords that visitors
use to search for your
site will help you
improve your site's
performance in
search engines. See
pages 173-4 for more.

**Traffic sources overview** The pie chart opposite reveals how visitors are finding your site, showing those who have reached it via a search engine, those who have followed a link from another site (called a 'referring site') and those who have simply entered your site's address directly into their browser (known as 'direct traffic'). Clicking on the chart reveals more detail, including the words and phrases that visitors have entered to search for your site on search engines such as Google itself.

**Content overview** This aspect of Analytics displays visitor statistics for the individual pages of your site. The most important pages should be drawing the biggest audiences. If not, consider whether your site's design is giving too much prominence to the least important content.

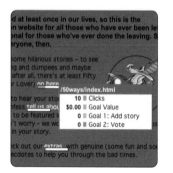

Site overlay shows the links on
your site that users are clicking
on, and exposes those they are
ignoring.

## Site Overlay

One of the most useful features of Google Analytics is arguably rather hidden from view. The Site Overlay opens your site in a new browser window and superimposes Analytics data about every link. As you browse your site, you can see exactly how effective each link is – and then tweak your design accordingly. To try this feature, click 'Content' in the left-hand menu and then choose 'Site Overlay'.

## Conversion goals

Another way to monitor the effectiveness of your site is to define the paths that you would like visitors to take as they move through your site, and then measure the number of people that actually do as you envisaged.

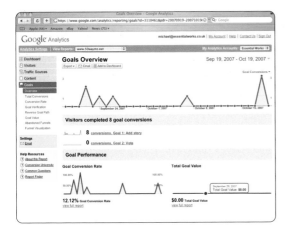

The Goals Overview page makes it easy to see whether your site is meeting its objectives.

Take the example of an online shop which has a special promotion on its homepage. The shop's website is designed to promote that item and then to allow purchasers to complete their transaction as swiftly as possible. The transaction is complete when the user arrives at a page that thanks them for their custom.

Reaching this page is known as a 'conversion', and with Google Analytics, the site's owners are able to map out every stage of the path (or 'funnel') that leads to the conversion page. This not only allows the shop to count how many conversions its site is generating, but also reveals how many potential customers fail to complete purchases. What's more, it lets the site's owners know at exactly which stage of the process (which page in the funnel) this failure has occurred. That page can then be modified in the hope of increasing the site's conversion rate.

To get started with goals in Google Analytics, click on 'Goals' in the menu on the left-hand side of the page.

# Search engine optimization

With the vast majority of web users turning to the likes of Google, Yahoo! and Live Search to find anything online, the birth of the search engine optimization consultant should come as no surprise. But you don't necessarily need professional help to boost your site's search engine rankings.

**must know**

Most search engines now divide their results into sponsored links – from which the search engine earns money from site owners – and organic results. The information in this section relates to organic search. Find out more about sponsored results on pages 178–9.

## How search engines work

Search engines attempt to use their knowledge of online content to match search terms entered by their users with relevant web pages. To include a site in the result, the search engine must previously have read that site's content and indexed it in its database. Site owners can either ask search engines to index their sites, or wait for the search engine's automated 'robot' to find the site for itself. These robots are constantly 'crawling' the web in search of new and updated sites.

The order in which sites appear in search engine results is the product of a complicated calculation that balances a number of different factors, some of which are discussed below. It's almost impossible to say which factors carry the most weight, since search engines – anxious to protect their results from manipulation – keep the details of their various calculations a closely guarded secret. They even make periodic adjustments to their calculations to throw over-curious site owners off the trail. That said, it's safe to say that search engines are all focused on delivering relevant results, so making your site more relevant to particular search terms will always be a sensible strategy.

## The good news

By designing your site using CSS, you have already gone a long way towards optimizing it for the search engine robots. Stripped of extraneous presentational mark-up, your site's XHTML pages are the concentrated nuggets of pure content that search engines love. Using heading levels to structure content and including relevant page titles, link titles and alternative text for images will also have helped search engines to understand your site and associate it with the kind of search terms its target audience are likely to be looking for.

## The bad news

Unfortunately, optimizing your site for search engines can be a rather inexact science. Even the sites that appear at the very top of the search results are always looking over their shoulder, since a change in the search engine's calculation or the arrival of a new, better-optimized competitor could be all it takes to throw a once top performer to a position of relative obscurity. Getting to the top of the pile is a battle won, but staying there is a war that never ends.

## Practical ways to optimize your site

In addition to sound, well-structured code, the techniques below should help to optimize your site for search engines.

### Research and use keywords

Search engines are primarily focused on sites' textual content, so choose the words you use carefully. Copy should be clear and to the point. Don't write an

Most visits to websites are referred from search engines, and some site owners go to great lengths to ensure their pages appear prominently.

Keyword tools like Wordtracker can help you identify the phrases likely to be used to search for your site.

essay when a paragraph would suffice, but do aim for a high density of relevant keywords. Both Google and Yahoo! offer free keyword tools (at https://adwords.google.com/select/Keyword ToolExternal and http://inventory.overture.com /d/searchinventory/suggestion respectively), which suggest keywords associated with a given topic and show the number of searches that have been carried out using those terms in the last year. Wordtracker (wordtracker.com) is another great site for keyword generation – you will have to pay for the full service, but there is also a free, scaled-down version (see http://freekeywords.wordtracker.com).

### Landing pages

Identifying the keywords and phrases most often used to search for information about the content on your site allows you to tailor the presentation of your content to match these searches more precisely. By improving the relevancy of your web pages to specific search queries, you increase the chances of your page appearing higher up the search engine's results. Landing pages are the pages of your site – often not the homepage – upon which visitors first enter your site. Creating landing pages whose content is carefully focused on a specific search term can be a key technique to pull visitors to your site via search engines.

## Title tags

Making sure that the title of each page on your site (entered between the `<title>` and `</title>` tags of each XHTML document) is specific to that page's content has already been mentioned. To improve page titles further, develop a naming convention that incorporates not only the content of the specific page, but also – if your site is big enough – the section to which that page belongs and the name of the site itself. Designers often use the pipe symbol (|) or arrow (>) on your keyboard to separate different parts of a title.

**try this**

Use the search engines to search for the phrases you want your site to be associated with, and visit the sites that are currently at the top of the list. You may be surprised at the results: if the sites that come up don't really answer the search you entered, there could be a hole for your site to fill. If, on the other hand, competition is furious, consider focusing your efforts on more specific search terms.

Use page titles that not only identify the content of a page but also reflect its position in your site's hierarchy.

**must know**

Meta tags do provide an effective way of *preventing* your pages appearing in search engine results. Add `<meta name="robots" content="noindex, nofollow">` to the head section of an XHTML document to stop robots indexing that page or following any links contained within it. For greater control use a robots.txt file (see www.robotstxt.org).

## Meta tags

Like the page title, meta tags belong within the head section of an XHTML document. Their content is not shown in the main browser window, but can be read by search engine robots. The meta description tag shown below is particularly interesting, since some search engines use its content to describe that page in its listings:

```
<meta name="description" content="The
Camden Canteen menu page, featuring our
fresh, organic dishes and examples of
our seasonal daily specials." />
```

However, the importance of meta tags has declined of late, and they are now largely ignored by many search engines. Adding meta tags to your web pages will do no harm, but avoid making them the cornerstone of your online marketing campaign.

## Reciprocal links

One of the ways that search engines rate the importance of a web page to a specific topic is the number of other web pages that link to it. Research other sites that are relevant to your own pages and contact the site owners to see if they would be willing to place a link to your page on their site. In return, you could offer to link back to their site. Think quality as well as quantity. Search engines attach less importance to links from pages whose content is not truly relevant to the target page.

It's easy to focus all your attention on the biggest search engines, but smaller ones and niche

directories are not to be sniffed at – they can still send significant numbers of visitors your way. Visitors referred from relevant niche sites are also more likely to belong to your target audience. For a commercial site, this could translate into more sales.

**Search engines use the number of relevant external websites that link to your page as a guide to its importance. For a restaurant, online reviews with links to the restaurant's homepage are ideal.**

## Get real
Be realistic in your expectations, and try to look at your site as the search engine sees it. If you are the owner of a hotel in England, your site will never be more relevant to a search for English hotels than an online directory that lists *all* the hotels in England. Your time might be better spent ensuring that your hotel's site is prominent on the directory.

Finally, be patient. Some search engines treat new sites with scepticism, and your ranking may improve once your site has demonstrated its longevity.

### try this
For a list of sites that are already linking to your site, enter link: followed by your website address (for example link:www.camdencanteen.com) into Google.

# Sponsored search

Paying your way to the top of the search engine results seems like an easy way to attract more visitors to your site. In recent years, pay-per-click (PPC) advertising has become a core revenue stream for all the main search engines.

## How it works

When you search for something on any of the leading search engines, sponsored results usually appear above and to the side of the main listings. Click on one of the sponsored results, and the search engine earns a small commission from the site owner. This is pay-per-click advertising.

Though some users are suspicious of sponsored search results, the search engines argue that the system serves everyone's interests: users are only shown adverts that are relevant to the search term they entered, site owners get direct exposure to the people looking for their products and services, and search engines make the profits that help fund the free services they provide.

The biggest pay-per-click advertising schemes are Google Adwords, Yahoo! Sponsored Search and Microsoft adCenter.

**Google Adwords**

Google Adwords (www.google.co.uk/adwords) is the most well-known PPC scheme, although it's based on technology licensed from a company now owned by Yahoo! As well as the sponsored results that appear in Google's own search results, Google

**must know**

Search engines sometimes distribute free vouchers for their PPC advertising schemes. Such schemes represent a great way to experiment with PPC advertising. Look out for the adverts in business and web design magazines. Many web hosting companies also include PPC vouchers as part of their hosting packages.

Adwords links also appear on a large network of other sites, and next to messages viewed using Google's web-based email service, Google mail.

### Yahoo! Sponsored Search

Like Adwords, Yahoo! Sponsored Search (http://searchmarketing.yahoo.com) generates adverts that appear both on Yahoo!'s own search engine results and across a network of partner sites.

### Microsoft adCenter

Advertising placed through Microsoft's adCenter (https://adcenter.microsoft.com) currently appears on Microsoft's Live Search search engine, and will also be shown on other Microsoft-owned websites and partner websites.

# Buying PPC advertising

Though there are differences between the various PPC schemes, the basic process for buying advertising is common to all. Advertisers first identify the search terms they would like to associate with their site, and then set the amount of money they are willing to spend each time their advert is clicked upon. This figure, combined with the search engine's assessment of an advert's relevancy to the search query, determine how prominently the advert is displayed. Advertisers can also set a daily budget for the total amount of money they are willing to spend. For example, if you pay 10p for every click and set a daily budget of £1, your advert will no longer appear once it has received ten clicks in one day.

**Visually, sponsored results are clearly separated from the main listings. Contextually, however, the two are closely related.**

**must know**

Choosing a pay-per-click amount is a bidding process. You can use the search engine's keyword tools combined with a degree of trial and error to get an idea of the popularity of different terms, and estimate how much you will have to bid for your advert to appear higher in the results. But don't focus all your attention on budget: relevance is important too.

# Running adverts on your site

Selling advertising space on your web pages can be an easy way to earn money from your site, and finding well-known advertisers is surprisingly straightforward.

**Advertising is a major part of this big commercial site, and affiliate schemes make it easy to include similar ads on your own pages.**

## Advertising sales made easy

Most website owners don't have the time or resources to sell advertising space to individual advertisers. If this applies to your site, the schemes below could solve the problem. Both will bring the advertisers to you, and make it easy to integrate their adverts in your code.

### Affiliate schemes

Websites with their own affiliate schemes recruit partner sites (affiliates) to advertise their products. The affiliate scheme provides all the adverts, as well as the code that affiliates must add to their pages in order to run them. Affiliates receive a small royalty for featuring the adverts, and are able to manage the entire process – from choosing ads to monitoring the revenue they generate – online.

The online bookseller Amazon and the Hilton chain of hotels are just two examples of companies with their own affiliate schemes, and many more familiar brands operate similar schemes through intermediary sites such as TradeDoubler (www.tradedoubler.com) and Commission Junction (www.cj.com). These sites allow you to apply to multiple affiliate schemes, and you can start adding the ads to your site as soon as each advertiser has approved your application.

## Google AdSense

Google's AdSense programme allows you to add your web pages to the network of sites that display adverts generated by the AdWords scheme discussed above. Unlike the colourful graphics generally provided by affiliate schemes, AdSense adverts are entirely text-based. Putting them on your site is a simple matter of adding a few extra lines of code – provided by Google – to your pages' mark-up. In typical Google style, the focus is on contextual relevance: Google scans the content of your pages and makes sure the ads it provides are likely to appeal to your site's core audience. You earn a commission when a user clicks on one of the AdSense adverts on your site. The exact amount will depend on how much the advertiser has bid to appear on your site in the first place.

The content of this camcorder review site is interspersed with related adverts, provided by Google AdSense.

# Enhancing accessibility

Using XHTML and CSS to separate the content of your site from its presentation is in itself the cornerstone of an accessible website. In this section, you will find out how accessible your site already is and learn how to enhance it even further.

**The W3C Web Accessibility Initiative site (www.w3.org/WAI) is a mine of useful information.**

## Accessibility comes as standard

An accessible website is one whose content can be accessed, understood and navigated by everyone, irrespective of issues such as the hardware or software they are using or any disability they may have. Creating a truly accessible site is a laudable aim, but translating good intentions into a working website is not always as easy as it sounds. To make things easier, the W3C's accessibility guidelines prioritize the different steps you can take to enhance your site's accessibility. There are three levels of priority, with priority 1 items being the most important. Read the W3C's recommendations for improving accessibility (www.w3.org/TR/WCAG10-CORE-TECHS).

### Reviewing your site

If you have followed the techniques in this book, you have already implemented many of the W3C's priority 1 and 2 accessibility criteria. These include:

● Structuring your content with valid, semantic XHTML and controlling its presentation with valid CSS. Keeping content and presentation separate means that the content of your site can be presented in different ways according to the varying circumstances of different users.

- Not relying on colour alone to convey your information. On the Camden Canteen site, the fact that hyperlinks are underlined makes them visible to users who are unable to distinguish them from surrounding text by their different colour.
- Using alternative text for images, so that users unable to see graphics can still understand their meaning, and avoiding graphical text.
- Ensuring that all the text on your site is legible, concise and appropriate to your site's subject matter.
- Taking care to avoid graphics that may trigger seizures for sufferers of photosensitive epilepsy.
- Including meta tags in the head element of your site's pages.
- Maintaining a consistent layout across your site and using a consistent navigation device to help users find their way around.

## Additional steps

Once you have taken care of the basics, consider any extra measures you could take to enhance your site's accessibility even further. Most of the techniques listed below are simple to implement, and some offer the added bonus of enhancing your site's visibility to search engines.

### Create a sitemap page

A sitemap is simply a page of your site that lists all its content, organized by section and with a hyperlink to each individual page. Sitemaps provide a clear overview of your site's structure, and make it easy for users and search engine robots to understand and navigate its content.

**This sitemap is clear and well structured. It helps humans and search engine robots alike.**

**Add skiplinks to every page**

Sites built around a common page template inevitably result in content such as the site's name and navigation links becoming repetitive. Though providing this content on every page is a requirement of an accessible site, the repetition can become irritating to users already familiar with your site's structure. This is especially true of users accessing your site with screen-reading software, who may be forced to listen to lengthy navigation options every time they open a new page. Skiplinks, placed shortly after the opening <body> tag of every page on your site, address this by allowing users to jump straight to the main content of the page – bypassing items such as the main navigation. The code for a skiplink is the same as that for an ordinary hyperlink, except that the value of the href attribute is not the address of another page but a location on the current page. The code below, for example, could be used to add a basic skiplink to our sample site. Here, #main refers to the unique id of the main content division:

```
<p><a href="#main">Skip to main content
</a></p>
```

## Access keys

Browsing the web relies heavily on using a mouse or trackpad to move around the screen, scroll up and down pages and click on links. This comes as second nature to most users, but can be a real struggle for groups such as the visually-impaired. Adding XHTML's accesskey attribute to anchor tags is intended to aid these users by providing a keyboard shortcut that opens the link with which it is

**must know**

Some designers use CSS to move skiplinks outside the visible area of the browser window, thus targetting them only at users employing screen-reading software to access your site. For more on this technique, see http://css-discuss. incutio.com/?page= ScreenreaderVisibility

**did you know?**

Though there is no agreed convention relating to the assignment of access keys, 0 is often used as a keyboard shortcut to a site's accessibility statement.

associated. The code below, for example, makes the 's' key a shortcut for this skiplink:

```
<p class=skiplink><a href="#main" access
key="s">Skip to main content</a></p>
```

Unfortunately, access keys can also cause problems. They work differently in different browsers and can conflict with browsers' own shortcuts. As it is impractical to associate a keyboard shortcut with every link, it is probably best to limit their application to skiplinks and selected key pages.

## Make an accessibility statement

An accessibility statement is a page of your site that details the ways in which you have tried to enhance its accessibility and explains how users can exploit these features. If you have set up access keys, it is important to list all keyboard shortcuts used.

## CSS image replacement

Ideally, your site should not use graphical text where plain text would suffice. If graphical text cannot be avoided, try using a CSS image-replacement technique. These use CSS to display the graphic as a background image, leaving live text in the XHTML document. Further CSS is then used to position the live text outside the main area of the screen, so that only the background image is visible in the browser window (find out more at www.mezzoblue.com/tests/revised-image-replacement).

Now that you've done all you can to maximize your site's accessibility, it's time to sit back and welcome visitors to your site. Well done and good luck!

**want to know more?**

• Read the latest search engine gossip at www.searchengine watch.com
• For a light-hearted but nonetheless informative overview of the trials and tribulations of improving your site's performance on search engines, visit www.meangene.com/google/design_for_google.html
• For an excellent guide to web accessibility see the website of The Royal National Institute of Blind People. Find it at www.rnib.org.uk/xpedio/groups/public/documents/code/public_rniboo8789.hcsp
• WebXACT (webxact.watchfire.com) is a free, automated service that examines your site and highlights potential accessibility problems.

# Glossary

**Accessibility** Quality that describes how easily a site can be accessed by the widest possible audience.

**Affiliate scheme** Program by which site owners ('affiliates') receive a royalty when an advert on their website is clicked upon or results in a sale.

**Attribute** Section of XHTML code within an element's opening tag, giving the browser extra information associated with that element.

**Bandwidth** The network capacity used to download your site to users' browsers.

**Blog** Short for 'web log' – an online journal.

**Box model** Theoretical model describing the interaction of the CSS margin, padding and border properties.

**Browser-safe fonts** Fonts that come pre-installed on most computers.

**Cascade** The hierarchy that determines the relative importance of different rules in a CSS document.

**Class** Selector in a CSS document that can be applied to multiple XHTML elements.

**Code editor** Enhanced text editor whose extra features make writing code easier.

**CMS** Content management system, used to edit the content of a dynamic website via a browser.

**CSS** Cascading Style Sheets, used to format a website's content.

**Dithering** The simulation of colours using a pattern of other colours.

**Doctype** The specific standard of XHTML according to which an XHTML document is displayed and validated.

**Domain** Component of a website address, referring to a specific sphere of the internet.

**Dynamic website** Site whose pages are generated using content returned from an online database.

**Favicon** Graphical icon associated with a specific website. Short for 'favourites icon'.

**Fixed-width layout** A page whose horizontal width is set in absolute units.

**Fluid layout** A page whose horizontal width is set in relative units.

**FTP client** Software to transfer files between different computers using File Transfer Protocol.

**GIF** Graphics Interchange Format, a file format used to save simple graphics and animations for the web.

**Graceful degradation** Characteristic of sites that remain useable even when the software used to view them does not exploit all the site's features.

**Graphics application** Software used to create and edit images and photos.

**IP address** Numerical Internet Protocol address unique to every web server.

**Host** The server on which a website is stored, or the company to whom the server belongs.

**JPEG** Joint Photographic Experts Group file format, used to save photographs for display online.

**Landing page** The first page of your site viewed by a specific visitor, often not your homepage.

**Linux** Computer operating system that is often used to run web servers.

**On-the-fly** Describes website pages that are generated as a result of querying a database.

**Organic results** Search engine listings that are not influenced by advertisers.

**PNG** Portable Network Graphic, another file format for web graphics.

**PPC** Pay-per-click search engine results, where advertisers pay every time a user clicks on their listing.

**Property** The formatting characteristic set by a CSS rule, such as font or colour.

**Pseudo-class** Appendage to the selector in a

CSS document used to create different styles for different states of the user's activity.

**RAM** Random Access Memory, used by personal computers to function smoothly.

**Registrar** Agent licensed to sell domain names.

**Robot** Computer which indexes websites for inclusion in search engine listings. Also known as a 'spider' or 'crawler'.

**Screen resolution** Measure of the number of pixels in a computer monitor setting, and therefore of the available space in which to display a website.

**SEO** Search engine optimization, the practice of tweaking web pages in the hope of improving their prominence in search engine results.

**Selector** The part of a CSS rule that specifies which XHTML code the rule affects.

**Server** Remote computer from which internet users download your website.

**Sitemap** Hierarchical list or chart showing the interrelationship of every page on a site.

**Skiplink** Link near the beginning of an XHTML document which allows users to jump straight to the main page content, bypassing repeated elements such as the site navigation.

**Social networking sites** Sites that connect individual personal profiles to form an online network of friends.

**Tag** Labels that mark the beginning and end of an element in XHTML code.

**Text editor** Basic software used to write text, including computer code.

**TLD** Top level domain such as .com or .fr, which forms the last part of a website address.

**Traffic** Collective term for all visits to a website.

**URL** Uniform Resource Locator. Technical name for the address of a web page or website.

**Validation** Procedure to highlight errors in XHTML and CSS code.

**Web 2.0** Controversial term used to describe a new breed of website seen as breaking the boundaries of what has previously been achieved online.

**Value** Formatting option chosen for a particular property in a CSS rule, such as red or bold.

**Web-safe colours** Palette of 216 solid colours common to both Windows and Macintosh operating systems.

**WYSIWYG editor** Editor whose graphical interface promises that What You See Is What You Get.

**W3C** The Worldwide Web Consortium, a body which develops standards for web development.

**XHTML** Extensible HyperText Markup Language, used to communicate the content of a website to the browser.

## Key to code colours

### XHTML code

**Green** anchor tags and their associated attributes

**Purple** image tags and their associated attributes

**Aqua** table tags and their associated attributes

**Dark blue** all other element tags and their associated attributes

**Mid-blue** values of attributes

**Grey** comments

**Black** live text that will actually appear in the browser window

### CSS code

**Magenta** selectors

**Dark blue** properties

**Mid-blue** values

**Grey** comments

# Need to know more?

## Further reading

*Beginning CSS Web Development: From Novice to Professional* by Simon Collison, Apress (2006)
*Search Engine Optimization: An Hour a Day* by Jennifer Grappone and Gradiva Couzin, Sybex (2006)
*The Google Story* by David A. Vise, Pan Books (2006)

## Useful websites

### General advice

**SitePoint** www.sitepoint.com

### XHTML and CSS

456 Berea Street
www.456bereastreet.com
A List Apart
www.alistapart.com
CSS Basics
www.cssbasics.com
How to Create
www.howtocreate.co.uk
Juicy Studio
www.juicystudio.com
MaxDesign
http://css.maxdesign.com.au
meyerweb.com
www.meyerweb.com
.net magazine
www.netmag.co.uk
smackthemouse
www.smackthemouse.com
The WellStyled Workshop
www.wellstyled.com
W3C Schools
www.w3schools.com

Web Design From Scratch
www.webdesignfromscratch.com
Web Start Center
www.webstartcenter.com/howto

### Design and graphics

BestWebGallery
http://bestwebgallery.com
csstux
www.csstux.com
DarkEye
www.dark-i.com
Design Melt Down
www.designmeltdown.com
Design Shack
www.designshack.co.uk
Design Snack
www.designsnack.com
design|snips
www.designsnips.com
Favicon.ico Generator
www.favicon.cc
High Floater
www.highfloater.com
strangefruits
www.strangefruits.nl
The Best Designs
www.thebestdesigns.com
www.webtypography.net
Web Designer Wall
www.webdesignerwall.com
Web Design Library
www.webdesign.org

### Search engine optimization

Organic SEO Wiki
www.organicseo.org

SEO Book
www.seobook.com
SEO Browser
www.seo-browser.com
Your SEO Plan
www.yourseoplan.com

### Advertising

Amazon Associates
https://affiliate-program.amazon.co.uk
Commission Junction
www.cj.com
Google AdSense
www.google.co.uk/adsense
Trade Doubler
www.tradedoubler.com
Google AdSense
www.google.co.uk/adsense

### Accessibility

Accessibility in Focus
www.accessibilityinfocus.co.uk
Accessites.org
http://accessites.org
HiSoftware Cynthia Says
www.cynthiasays.com
Web Standards Awards
http://webstandardsawards.com
Web Standards Project
http://webstandards.org
WebXACT
http://webxact.watchfire.com
W3C Web Content Accessibility Guidelines 1.0
www.w3.org/TR/WAI-WEB CONTENT

# Index

# Acknowledgements

For Eric, and for my family

Special thanks to all at Essential, especially Fiona and Nina (for guidance, patience and all-round finesse), Dipli (for perfectionism, sympathy and coffee with warm milk), and John (for the opportunity). Thanks also to Martin (for a proper job), Andy (for balance and technical prowess) and Natasha (for being on Facebook).

# ◌ Collins need to know?

**Look out for these recent titles in Collins' practical and accessible need to know? series.**

## Other titles in the series:

**To order any of these titles, please telephone 0870 787 1732 quoting reference 263H. For further information about all Collins books, visit our website: www.collins.co.uk**

# DEAN CLOSE SCHOOL

## LIBRARY

This book must be returned by the latest date stamped below.